EFFECTIVE WRITING:
A Handbook
for Accountants

Claire B. Arevalo

Consultant for Written Communications
J. M. Tull School of Accounting
University of Georgia

Library of Congress Cataloging in Publication Data

Arevalo, Claire.
  Effective writing.

  Includes bibliographical references and index.
  1. English language—Business English.   2. Accounting—
Language.   I. Title.
PE1116.A3A8   1984   808'.066657   83-19249
ISBN 0-13-246513-2 (P)
     0-13-246521-3 (C)

Editorial/production supervision and interior design: Pam Price
Cover design: Lundgren Graphics, Ltd.
Manufacturing buyer: Ray Keating

Printed in the United States of America

10 9 8 7 6 5 4 3 2 1

ISBN 0-13-246513-2 {P}

ISBN 0-13-246521-3 {C}

Prentice-Hall International, Inc., *London*
Prentice-Hall of Australia Pty. Limited, *Sydney*
Editora Prentice-Hall do Brasil, Ltda., *Rio de Janeiro*
Prentice-Hall Canada Inc., *Toronto*
Prentice-Hall of India Private Limited, *New Delhi*
Prentice-Hall of Japan, Inc., *Tokyo*
Prentice-Hall of Southeast Asia Pte. Ltd., *Singapore*
Whitehall Books Limited, *Wellington, New Zealand*

CONTENTS

PREFACE

Effective Writing: A Handbook for Accountants is designed to help accounting students and practitioners improve their writing skills. It can be used as a supplementary text for regular accounting courses, or as a text in a business communications or technical writing course when these courses include accounting students. The handbook is also a useful desk reference or self-study manual for accounting professionals.

Effective Writing guides the writer through all the stages of the writing process: initial planning, including analysis of audience and purpose; organizing the material; writing the rough draft; and revising for effective style and correct grammar. In addition to these basic writing principles, the book includes chapters on letters, memorandums, reports, and other formats used by accountants in actual practice.

Most chapters include exercises and writing topics for self-testing and practice. These assignments, like the illustrations in the text, deal with accounting concepts and situations, and thus will seem more relevant and interesting to men and women involved in the study and practice of accounting.

One way to use *Effective Writing* is in conjunction with regular accounting courses. Instructors can assign cases and topics for research based on the accounting concepts actually being studied in class, or use the assignments provided by this handbook. Students then analyze the accounting problem, research the literature if necessary, and prepare their answers according to an assigned format such as a technical memorandum or a formal report for a hypothetical client. The handbook will guide the students toward effective organization, style, format, grammar, and other elements of the writing process. Instructors can then evaluate the papers on the basis of accounting content and effective communication.

As a self-study manual, *Effective Writing* will help accounting professionals master the techniques of successful writing in the business world. The book contains numerous examples and practical applications of the techniques discussed. In addition, many chapters have exercises, with answers, which will enable the reader to practice the principles. A thoughtful review of *Effective Writing,* then, will give practicing accountants greater confidence in the writing situations that they encounter as part of their professional responsibilities.

Most of the material in *Effective Writing* has been used successfully for over five years at the J. M. Tull School of Accounting at the University of Georgia, which has pioneered in its writing program for accounting students.

The handbook covers the writing problems most frequently encountered by accounting students and practitioners, as demonstrated by extensive classroom testing and research into the communication needs of the profession. It is not intended to answer *all* questions of organization, style, or grammar, but it addresses the ones asked most frequently.

I wish to thank all the people who have helped me prepare this book:

- Professor Jay M. Smith, Institute of Professional Accountancy, Brigham Young University, for reviewing and testing the manuscript
- Professor Geraldine Kruse, Department of Accounting and Finance, Eastern Michigan University, for reviewing the manuscript
- Professor Robert W. Ingram, College of Business Administration, University of Iowa, for reviewing the manuscript
- Professors Herbert E. Miller, James Don Edwards, and Gordon S. May, and all the faculty and staff at the J. M. Tull School of Accounting, University of Georgia
- Kathy Wright, Patsy Heil, Robbie Strickland, Helen Wenner, and Gayle Miller, who also teach Business Communication
- Evelyn Lapp, Anna Marie Soper, Lin Young, Debbie Couch, Beatrice London, and Rosie Richardson, who helped me prepare the manuscript
- Jack Ochs, Elinor Paige, Pam Price, and Martha McDonald of Prentice-Hall.

I also want to thank my family for their love and encouragement.

Chapter 1

WHY EFFECTIVE WRITING IS IMPORTANT

Many accountants have recently become concerned about the need for effective writing skills. Multinational accounting firms now offer special courses to help their accountants write better. Various accounting organizations—the AICPA and state societies, for example—offer continuing professional education courses in writing. Many schools and departments of accounting now stress effective writing in accounting coursework.

Why all this interest in writing? To be truly competent, accountants must be able to use words effectively. In a study published by the AICPA, Robert H. Roy and James H. MacNeill stressed dramatically the importance of effective accounting communication:

> To the CPA the ability to express himself well is more than the hallmark of an educated man, it is a professional necessity. Inability to express his findings in understandable, explicit, unambiguous, intelligible English can be self-defeating, potentially misleading, and possibly disastrous to clients, creditors, and investors. . . . We feel justified, therefore . . . in being unequivocal about this requirement of the common body of knowledge for beginning CPAs: *candidates who cannot write the English language at least as well as a minimum-threshold should be denied admission to the profession, if need be on this account alone.*[1]

The American Accounting Association's Committee to Prepare a Statement of Basic Accounting Theory also identified the importance of communication in the practice of accounting: "Communication is a vital link in accounting activity. It is of no less importance than that of developing the information itself."[2]

So the ability to communicate effectively—whether in speaking or writing—is essential to success in the accounting profession. Unfortunately, many students and accountants lack the basic skills they need to be effective communicators.

THE PROBLEM

In a recent study sponsored by the American Accounting Association, Robert W. Ingram and Charles R. Frazier identified twenty communication skills important to the successful practice of accounting. A disturbing finding of the study was that *entry-level staff and accounting students are woefully deficient in most of these skills.*[3]

Of the skills identified by Ingram and Frazier, the following relate directly or indirectly to effective writing:[4]

* correspondence writing
* memorandums and informal report writing
* formal report writing
* correct grammar
* correct punctuation
* correct spelling
* outline development
* inductive reasoning
* deductive reasoning
* coherence
* clarity
* conciseness
* paragraph development
* use of visual aids

Accountants need these skills almost daily to communicate important information—through letters and reports, memorandums, and narrative sections of financial statements.

FINANCIAL STATEMENTS

Some portions of financial statements are written in narrative, rather than numerical, form. For instance, footnote disclosures communicate information that users may need to interpret the statements accurately. Here is an example of a footnote disclosure on a financial statement:[5]*

Summary of Principal Accounting Policies—
Principles Applied in Consolidation
  The consolidated financial statements include the accounts of U.S. Steel and its majority-owned subsidiaries except for those engaged in leasing and finance activities, which are carried at U.S. Steel's equity in their net assets plus advances.
  Investments in other affiliated companies in which U.S. Steel has significant influence in the management and control are accounted for using the equity method of accounting. They are carried in the investment account at the Corporation's share of the unit's net worth. The proportionate share of income from equity investments is included in Other income.
  Investments in marketable equity securities are carried at the lower of cost or market and other investments in companies owned are carried at cost with income recognized when dividends are received.

This footnote is fairly easy to understand. Unfortunately, the meaning of some footnote disclosures is not always clear to the average financial statement reader. Arthur Adelberg and Richard Lewis, in a recent article in the *Journal of Accountancy,* note the need for more clearly written footnotes. They suggest, for instance, that accountants use shorter sentences, active verbs, and definitions of technical terms when writing footnotes and other narrative portions of financial statements.[6]

LETTERS AND REPORTS

Many times accountants communicate information to clients through letters or reports. For example, engagement letters put into writing the arrangements made between an accounting firm and a client. Tax accountants in public practice often write letters to advise clients about the proper treatment of a tax problem. And an auditor, following an auditing engagement, often writes letters to the client suggesting ways to improve the client's business.

  Reports, both formal and informal, are also important ways to communicate accounting information. For instance, an accountant working for a corporation may write a report for management on alternative accounting treatments for a particular kind of business transaction.

  To be effective, letters and reports must be well written. How will clients react if, after reading a letter from their CPA, they are still confused about their income tax problem? How will management feel about a report that is poorly organized and hard to follow?

MEMORANDUMS

Sometimes accountants working within a firm, particularly a large firm, need to communicate with one another. For example, one member of a firm may interview a client about an accounting problem that will later be researched by other members of the staff. The interviewer will record the pertinent information on a memo for the client's file. Other individuals will later consult the memo to find the information needed to complete the research.

Effective memos are also an essential part of the working papers that accompany an audit. The auditor must be able to describe with clarity and precision the procedures he or she followed in the audit, the client's accounting policies and procedures, and the specific conclusions reached as a result of the auditing investigations. Thus accurate, complete, and understandable written documentation is part of the auditor's responsibility.

Memos also relate administrative information about the accounting firm itself—announcements of upcoming meetings, for example, or changes in firm policy.

* * * * *

In conclusion, accountants need writing skills for many of their routine, professional tasks, whether communicating with investors, management, clients, or fellow professionals. They need to use words effectively and to combine these words into good sentences and paragraphs. It is important to remember that accounting is a process of measuring and *communicating* information.

Writing skills pay off in professional advancement. Zane Robbins, of Arthur Andersen Co., notes:[7]

> All other things being equal, the professional accountant who can communicate best is likely to progress fastest. Those who are unable to write and communicate effectively often find themselves consigned to the purgatory of technician with little hope for long-term growth.

To succeed professionally, accountants must master many skills. They must understand and be able to apply accounting principles, of course, but they must also be able to communicate effectively. A competent accountant who is also an effective writer will usually be rewarded with professional success.

NOTES

1. Robert H. Roy and James H. MacNeill, *Horizons for a Profession: The Common Body of Knowledge for Certified Public Accountants* (New York: American Institute of Certified Public Accountants, 1967), pp. 218–19.
2. Committee to Prepare a Statement of Basic Accounting Theory, *A Statement of Basic Accounting Theory* (Evanston, Ill.: American Accounting Association, 1966), p. 13.
3. Robert W. Ingram and Charles R. Frazier, *Developing Communications Skills for the Accounting Profession* (Evanston, Ill.: American Accounting Association, 1980).
4. Ingram and Frazier, *Developing Communications Skills,* pp. 15–18.
5. *United States Steel Corporation 1980 Annual Report* (Pittsburgh, Pa.: United States Steel Corporation, 1980), p. 24.

6. Arthur Harris Adelberg and Richard A. Lewis, "Financial Reports Can Be Made More Understandable," *Journal of Accountancy,* 149 (June 1980): 44–50.

7. H. Zane Robbins, "How to Develop Basic Writing Skills," *The Chronicle,* 40, no. 1 (1981), 9.

EXERCISES

Exercise 1-1

Look for examples of effective and ineffective writing in the material you read regularly. Consider letters and memos you receive, as well as published professional material such as textbooks, professional articles, and FASB pronouncements. Then think about the following questions.

1. What kind of material do you find easiest to read? What are some of the qualities that make this writing readable?

2. Examine closely the writing you find difficult to read. How do you think the writing could be improved?

3. Make two lists of the specific qualities that make writing effective or ineffective. You might begin something like this:

EFFECTIVE WRITING	INEFFECTIVE WRITING
• shorter sentences	• long sentences
• shorter paragraphs	• long paragraphs
• conversational vocabulary	• too much jargon and "big words"
• correct grammar	• obvious grammatical mistakes
• etc.	• etc.

Exercise 1-2

Collect samples of your own writing, both professional and personal. Analyze your writing, considering the following questions.

1. What kind of response do you usually get to your writing from supervisors, peers, clients, and subordinates? Are readers sometimes uncertain of your meaning?

2. From the lists you made for Exercise 1-1, question 3, identify some of the strengths and weaknesses of your writing.

3. As you read this handbook and study the examples and exercises, look for ways you can improve your writing.

Chapter 2

THE WRITING PROCESS: AN OVERVIEW

Effective writing, like the accounting system, is a process. The first step in the accounting process is to analyze the transactions to determine how they should be treated. For example, the accountant decides where to record the transactions—what journals, ledgers, and accounts to use—and how detailed the entry descriptions must be in order to be useful.

Several questions basic to the accounting system underlie an accountant's analysis of financial transactions and their treatment. What is the purpose of the information recorded and ultimately reported? Who are the users of this information and what are their needs? How can this information be most fairly and effectively presented?

These questions are as important to good writing as they are to good accounting. Initial planning, emphasizing both the purpose of the writing and the needs of the readers, is the first step in the writing process.

INITIAL PLANNING:
ANALYZING THE PURPOSE
OF THE WRITING

A report on inventory flow assumptions could have numerous purposes. If you were writing such a report, you would first decide on its primary purpose. Should the report simply describe the various flow assumptions—LIFO, FIFO, average cost, etc.? Is the purpose of the report to recommend an inventory accounting treatment for a certain company in a given situation? Should the report analyze the potential problems arising from a change in flow assumptions—from FIFO to LIFO, perhaps?

There are many possible purposes for such a report, but the important idea is to analyze the purpose (or purposes) carefully *before* you begin to write. It might be helpful to think of purpose in terms of three basic categories: to give information about something, to propose a course of action, or to solve a problem. The purpose of most writing tasks will fall into one of these categories, or perhaps a combination of two or three.

Here's another example. Assume you are the controller for Eldorado Manufacturing. Eldorado is considering a purchase of stock from Western Materials, one of Eldorado's major suppliers of raw materials. A report on this possible purchase could have any of the following purposes:

- To inform management of the advantages (or disadvantages) of such a purchase
- To recommend that Eldorado purchase (or not purchase) the stock
- To suggest a way to finance the purchase

The purpose of the report, or of any writing, will determine what material it should contain. Consider another example. Your client is faced with a lawsuit that could result in a large loss. You might write a report for the client about the disclosure requirements for contingent loss liabilities due to pending litigation. In such a report you would not include a discussion of gain contingencies, nor a discussion of loss contingencies from bad debts. You would analyze the specific purpose of the report to decide what information was relevant for this situation.

It is a good idea to write down the purpose of your writing task before you begin further work on it. Be as specific and concrete as possible, and try to define your purpose within one sentence. This sentence will later become your thesis statement or statement of purpose. (These statements are discussed more fully in later chapters.)

INITIAL PLANNING:
ANALYZING THE READER

Another important consideration in the initial planning of a writing task is who the reader will be. A report dealing with a highly technical accounting topic would be written one way for a fellow accountant, but another way for a client with only a limited knowledge of accounting procedures and terminology.

Accountants are familiar with the concept of user needs in preparing financial statements. Likewise, effective writers analyze the needs of their readers. Of course, an accountant prepares financial statements for many users with a variety of needs and backgrounds. The writer of a report, letter, or memo usually writes for a limited number of people, or perhaps for only one person. Furthermore, a writer usually knows, or can find out, important information about the readers. Again, you must ask certain basic questions. How much knowledge do the readers have of the subject being discussed? The answer to this question will determine the terms that need defining or the procedures that need explaining.

Accountants dealing with the public should be particularly careful in analyzing the needs of their readers. For example, a tax specialist might have clients with widely varying experience and knowledge of taxation terminology. A corporation executive would probably understand such concepts as deferrals and loss carryforwards. But a small shopkeeper might not be familiar with these technical accounting terms and procedures. Business letters to these two clients, even on the same topic, would need to be written differently.

You may also need to consider the readers' attitudes and biases. Are they likely to be neutral to your recommendations, or will they need to be convinced? If you need to persuade your readers, remember to write with the readers' interests and needs in mind. How will the readers benefit, directly or indirectly, from what you propose? How can you present your arguments so that readers' objections and biases will be overcome? For this last question you will need to anticipate readers' questions, research the basic issues, and then organize your arguments into a convincing arrangement (see the following section).

Other important considerations when analyzing readers' needs are tone and style. Again, what are their attitudes and biases? Some readers react well to an informal, friendly style of writing, but other readers believe that professional writing should be more formal.

Consider also your word choices. If your reader is a woman, will she resent the following sentence?

> An efficient accountant dictates letters to his secretary; she then types the letters for his signature.

Some readers might argue that the choice of pronouns (accountant/he, secretary/she) implies a sexist bias. More traditional readers might not object to the sentence at all. (Note: this sentence can be revised to avoid the issue of sexism by using plural nouns: Efficient accountants dictate letters to their secretaries, who then type the letters for their supervisors' signature.)

But whoever your reader is, remember always to be courteous. Whether you write in a technical or simplified style, all readers appreciate (and deserve!) consideration, tact, and respect.

Analyzing reader needs is an important part of the preparation for writing. Initial planning, which considers both your audience and your purpose, is the first rule of effective writing:

1.   Analyze the purpose of the writing and the needs of the readers.

GETTING STARTED: THE OUTLINE

Once you have evaluated the purpose of the writing and the needs of the readers, you are ready for the second stage in the writing process: organizing the ideas you want to present. This step may be quick and simple. For a short letter you can list the three or four ideas you wish to include in the letter, perhaps one idea for each paragraph. On the other hand, a long letter or a report will require a more detailed outline.

In some situations, you may need to do some initial background reading before you can make your outline. If you are writing a research report on a technical topic, for example, you will need to survey the literature to identify the important aspects of the subject; these aspects will then become the major divisions of the outline. Chapter 11 discusses background reading, as well as other phases of the research process, in more detail.

Most outlines are organized in a complex-deductive structure: a main idea (the thesis statement or statement of purpose), major supports, and minor supports. See Chapter 4 and Chapter 7 for a further discussion of complex-deductive patterns of organization.

After you have made a list or outline of your important ideas, you can consider several questions. Does the outline cover the subject completely, or should you expand it to include other ideas? Does it include an idea that is not relevant to the purpose of the writing? Have you presented the ideas in the most effective order?

The order in which you present your ideas is an important consideration. To some extent the order will depend on the particular report, letter, etc., you are writing. However, several principles of good organization apply to all writing tasks.

First, nearly all writing has the same basic structure:

Introduction of the subject: provides background information, stresses the importance of the topic.

Concise statement of the main ideas, usually in one sentence: thesis statement, statement of purpose, topic sentence, etc. (See Chapter 3.)

Development of the main ideas: includes explanations, examples, analyses, steps, reasons, proofs. This part of an outline or paper is often called the body.

Conclusion: repeats the main idea and brings the paper to an effective close.

Later chapters of this handbook will discuss more fully this basic structure as it is used for particular kinds of writing.

Second, you can usually arrange the ideas in a logical order. For instance, if you were describing the process of reconciling bank statements, you would discuss each step of the procedure in the order in which it is performed.

Finally, you can often organize the ideas according to their importance. One approach is to progress from the most important to the least important points so that the report, letter, or other writing immediately catches and holds the reader's attention, and convinces the reader of the soundness of your arguments.

As an example, suppose you are writing a report to recommend that your firm purchase a new computer system for its accounting records. Naturally, you will want to emphasize the advantages of this purchase—describing them in the order that is likely to be most convincing *to the readers* of the report. However, an investment in a computerized accounting system might also have drawbacks—for example, the cost to purchase and install the equipment and the problems involved in converting to the new system. For your report to appear well researched and unbiased, you will need to include these disadvantages in your discussion—and, of course, in the outline as you are preparing the report. To organize your report, you might use the following basic structure:

> I. Introduction, including your recommendation
> II. Body
>   A. Advantages, beginning with those most appealing to the readers
>   B. Disadvantages, including, when possible, ways to minimize or overcome any drawbacks
> III. Conclusion

If you analyze your outline or list of ideas before you begin to write, you will be able to decide in advance how your thoughts can be presented most effectively. You will also know that you have covered the subject thoroughly, but eliminated unnecessary digressions. This time spent initially in organizing the writing task will save time and effort when you actually begin to write. By following the outline, you will always know what to say next.

The list of rules for effective writing can now be expanded:

1. **Analyze the purpose of the writing and the needs of the readers.**
2. **Use an outline to organize the ideas you want to present.**

WRITING THE ROUGH DRAFT

The third step in the writing process is the rough draft. The purpose of this step is to get the ideas down on paper in whatever form they come most easily. Spelling, punctuation, and style are not important in the rough draft. What is important is that you write the ideas down so that later you can polish and correct them.

When you work on your rough draft, follow the outline you have already prepared. However, you may decide to change the outline as you go, omitting some parts that no longer seem to fit, or adding other ideas that now seem necessary. Changing the outline is fine, because when you revise the rough draft later you can make sure your thoughts are still well organized.

REVISING THE ROUGH DRAFT

The final stage in the writing process is the revision of the rough draft. It is in this stage that you check your spelling and grammar and polish your style. Make a final check also to see that the ideas are effectively and completely presented.

You will need to revise most of your writing more than once—perhaps even three or four times. The key to revising is to let the writing get cold between revisions; a time lapse between readings will enable you to read more objectively what you have written—what you have actually said, instead of what you meant to say. Ideally, revisions should be at least a day apart.

The next five chapters of the handbook will discuss what to look for when putting your writing in final form.

Here, then, is a third rule for effective writing:

1. **Analyze the purpose of the writing and the needs of the readers.**
2. **Use an outline to organize the ideas you want to present.**
3. **Write the rough draft, and then revise it to make the writing polished and correct.**

NOTES

1. Gadis J. Dillon, "Writing Assignment for Intermediate Accounting" (unpublished class assignment, University of Georgia, 1982).
2. Ibid.

EXERCISES

Exercise 2-1

Among your business correspondents are the following people:

1. The controller of a large corporation—a fellow accountant.
2. A manager in a large corporation—educated and experienced in business, though not an accountant.
3. The owner/president of a medium-sized business (2,500 employees)—experienced in business, but with little formal education.
4. The new owner of a small business—little business education or experience.
5. The stockholders of a large corporation.
6. A bookkeeper under your supervision.

For each correspondent, which of the following terms or procedures would you *likely* need to explain, and in how much detail?

a. GAAP
b. FASB
c. LIFO
d. historical cost
e. lower of cost or market
f. earnings statement
g. owners' equity
h. quick ratio
i. accounts receivable
j. rent expense
k. double-entry bookkeeping
l. capital leases—accounting for lessee

Exercise 2-2

You have been hired as a special assistant to Sam Jones, the president of Bulldog Sales Company. Mr. Jones has little formal education, but is very astute about business matters and is an especially good salesperson. He calls you in and says, "Bulldog Sales Company is in the nice position of having excess cash on hand. I am considering investing that cash in some bonds issued in 1975 by Red and Black Company, but I see in the *Wall Street Journal* that those bonds are selling at only 60% of their maturity value. Does that mean they are especially risky? Assuming I do make this investment, what are the accounting implications? Write a memo to me that will answer these questions."[1]

Analyze the purpose of the memo that you will write to Mr. Jones. What topics should you include to answer his questions? Are the following topics relevant to the purpose of the memo? Why?

definition of a bond
reasons for investing excess cash
bond discounts: what they mean
bond premiums: what they mean
accounting for bond premiums
accounting for bond discounts

Exercise 2-3

The society of CPAs in your state is offering a continuing professional education seminar entitled "Effective Writing." You want your firm to give you released time to attend the seminar and you would like to have your expenses paid. Your supervisor, Carol Black, is unfamiliar with the seminar; you will need to convince her that your attendance would benefit the firm by making you a more effective employee. You need to write a memo to Mrs. Black explaining your request.[2]

1. What ideas and information should you include in the memo?
2. How could you arrange this information in an effective order? Write an outline; be careful to include all relevant details about the seminar and an adequate justification for your request.

Exercise 2-4

The board of directors of your company is considering a switch from the FIFO to the LIFO inventory flow assumption. You must write a report for the board explaining the implications of such a change.

1. What major topics should you cover in your report? Consider taxes, the financial statements, and any other relevant topics.
2. Analyze your audience. What background information are they likely to need?
3. How should you arrange the information in your report? Write an outline.

Exercise 2-5

As part of a public relations campaign, the CPA firm you work for has decided to publish a series of short (500–1,000 words) brochures explaining some basic accounting concepts and procedures. Many of the firm's clients own small businesses. Although these clients are experienced in business, most have little formal accounting education.

You will need to write the brochures so that the clients can understand them. On the other hand, you don't want to "talk down" to them or sound patronizing.

Consider the purpose and audience for these brochures; make outlines for the following topics.

1. cash vs. accrual accounting
2. inventory accounting
3. expense and revenue recognition
4. internal control of cash
5. accounting for inflation
6. the primary financial statements
7. regulation of the accounting profession: public vs. private sector
8. accounting for leases
9. the history of the accounting profession
10. the audit

ANSWERS TO EXERCISES

Answer, Exercise 2-1

1. l
2. a, b, c, d, e, h, l
3. a, b, c, d, e, g, h, k, l
4. a–l
5. a, b, c, d, e, h, k, l
6. a, b, c, d, e, g, h, l

Answer, Exercise 2-2

These topics would be relevant to Mr. Jones' questions about the Red and Black bonds:

bond discounts: what they mean
accounting for bond discounts

Note: You might need to include other topics in your memo, as well. For example, you might want to list other accounting implications of bond investments. And you should specifically answer Mr. Jones's question about the riskiness of the Red and Black bonds. You might include a brief discussion of risk when you explain bond discounts.

Answer, Exercise 2-3

Possible outline:

  I. Introduction
    A. Identify the seminar
    B. Make a specific request
 II. The seminar
    A. Where
    B. When
    C. Sponsorship
    D. Cost of seminar, including registration, travel, and living expenses.
(Note: You may have already provided some of this information for I.A. above. Don't repeat yourself.)
III. Why you should go. These reasons will vary. For example, the seminar should improve your writing in several ways:
    A. Instructions to subordinates
    B. Reports and proposals to supervisors
    C. Letters and reports to clients
IV. Conclusion

Chapter 3

THE FLOW OF THOUGHT: UNITY AND COHERENCE

Chapter 2 discussed how to organize your outline to include only relevant material and how to present your thoughts in an effective order. This chapter discusses additional techniques to improve unity and coherence (continuity of thought) —two essential characteristics of effective writing.

UNITY

The key to unified writing is to establish the main idea of each writing task. An office memo may contain only one paragraph, but that paragraph will have a central idea. A report may run to many pages, but it will still have a central idea or purpose, and possibly secondary purposes as well. It is important to decide on your main ideas before you begin writing, preferably before you begin your outline.

You should be able to summarize a main idea in one sentence. In a paragraph, this sentence is called the topic sentence. In longer writings involving more than two or three paragraphs, this sentence is often called the thesis statement. A report may have a thesis statement, a statement of purpose, or both.

The main idea is the key to the entire writing task. Every other sentence should be related to it, either directly or indirectly. The central idea is like the hub of a wheel or the trunk of a tree. All other ideas branch off from the central idea; they explain it, analyze it, illustrate it, or prove it. Any sentences that are unrelated to the main idea, either directly or indirectly, are irrelevant (off the subject) and should be omitted. In longer writings, entire paragraphs may be irrelevant to the main purpose; these irrelevant paragraphs are called digressions.

When you remove digressions and irrelevant sentences, you achieve unified writing: every sentence, either directly or indirectly, is related to the main idea.

The paragraph below is not unified. Which sentences do you think are irrelevant to the topic sentence?

(1) Incorporation offers many advantages for a business and its owners. (2) For example, the owners are not responsible for the business's debts. (3) Investors hope to make money when they buy stocks in a corporation. (4) Incorporation also enables a business to obtain professional management skills. (5) Corporations are subject to more government regulation than are other forms of organization.

Sentence 1, the topic sentence, identifies what should be the main idea of the paragraph: the advantages of incorporation. Sentences 3 and 5 are off the subject.

The concept of unity gives us the fourth rule for effective writing:

1. **Analyze the purpose of the writing and the needs of the readers.**
2. **Use an outline to organize the ideas you want to present.**
3. **Revise the rough draft to make the writing polished and correct.**
4. **Make the writing unified—all sentences should relate to the main idea, either directly or indirectly.**

COHERENCE

Coherence is writers' jargon for a smooth flow of ideas. Coherent writing is easy to follow. There are no jumps in thought; one sentence or paragraph flows logically into the next one. Another way of describing coherent writing is to say that the ideas show continuity.

Effective writers use four basic techniques to make their writing coherent. First, they arrange their ideas in a logical order. They work out the best order for the ideas as they plan the outline. They use three other techniques as they write or revise the rough draft. These additional techniques are the use of transitional expressions, the repetition of key words or phrases, and the use of pronouns.

Transitional Expressions

Transitions link ideas together. They can be used between sentences, paragraphs, and major divisions of the writing. Their purpose is to show the relationship between two ideas: how the second idea flows logically from the first, and how both are related to the main idea of the entire writing.

As an example of how transitions work, consider the following paragraph. The topic sentence (main idea) is the first sentence; the transitional expressions are in italics.

(1) Financial statements are important to a variety of users. (2) *First,* investors and potential investors use the statements to decide if a company is a good investment risk. (3) These users look at such factors as net income, the debt-to-equity ratio, and retained earnings. (4) *Second,* creditors use financial statements to decide if a firm is a good credit risk. (5) Creditors want to know if a firm has a large enough cash flow to pay its debts. (6) *Third,* governmental agencies analyze financial statements for a variety of purposes. (7) *For example,* the Internal Revenue Service will want to know if the company has paid the required amount of taxes on its income. (8) These examples of financial statement users show how diverse their interests can be.

The sentences beginning *first* (2), *second* (4), and *third* (6) give three examples of the paragraph's main idea: the variety of financial statement users. These three sentences relate to one another in a logical, sequential way, which the transitions make clear. These sentences also relate directly to the topic sentence; they illustrate it with specific examples. Sentence 7, which begins with *for example,* relates only indirectly to the main idea of the paragraph, but it relates directly to sentence 6. Sentence 7 expresses one example of the purposes financial statements have for government agencies.

Transitions can express a number of relationships between ideas. In the above paragraph, the transitions indicate an enumerated list (2, 4, and 6) and a specific illustration of a general statement (7). Transitions can also imply other relationships between ideas—conclusions, additional information, or contradiction, for example. On page 18 is a list of frequently used transitional expressions, their meanings, and example sentences showing how some of them work.

To illustrate further the importance of transitions within a paragraph, look at the following example, which lacks transitions.

Incorporation offers several advantages to businesses and their owners. Ownership is easy to transfer. The business is able to maintain a continuous existence even when the original owners are no longer involved. The stockholders of a corporation are not held responsible for the business's debts. If the XYZ Corporation defaults on a $1,000,000 loan, its investors will not be held responsible for paying that liability. Incorporation enables a business to obtain professional managers with centralized authority and responsibility. The business can be run more efficiently. Incorporation gives a business certain legal rights. It can enter into contracts, own property, and borrow money.

Now see how much easier it is to read the paragraph when it has appropriate transitions.

Incorporation offers several advantages to businesses and their owners. *For one thing,* ownership is easy to transfer, *and* the business is able to maintain a continuous existence even when the original owners are no longer involved. *In addition,* the stockholders of a corporation are not held responsible for the business's bad debts. *For example,* if the XYZ Corporation defaults on a $1,000,000 loan, its investors will not be held responsible for paying that liability. Incorporation *also* enables a business to obtain professional managers with centralized authority and responsibility; *therefore,* the business can be run more efficiently. *Finally,* incorporation gives a business certain legal rights. *For example,* it can enter into contracts, own property, and borrow money.

Transitional Words and Phrases

Adding a point or piece of information:
and, also, in addition, moreover, furthermore, first/second/third, finally
Accounting is a demanding profession. It can also be financially rewarding.

Making an exception or contrasting point:
but, however, nevertheless, on the other hand, yet, still, on the contrary, in spite of. . . , nonetheless
Historical cost accounting causes many problems. Nevertheless, it is still the basis of most accounting procedures.

Giving specific examples or illustrations:
for example, for instance, as an illustration, in particular, to illustrate
Financial statements serve a variety of users. For example, investors use them in evaluating potential investments.

Clarifying a point:
that is, in other words, in effect, put simply, stated briefly
The basic accounting equation is *assets equal liabilities plus owners' equity.* That is, A = L + OE.

Conceding a point to the opposite side:
granted that, it may be true that, even though, although
Although generally accepted accounting principles are not perfect, they offer considerable assurance that financial statements are presented fairly.

Indicating place, time, or importance:
Place: above, beside, beyond, to the right, below, around
Time: formerly, hitherto, earlier, in the past, before, at present, now, today, these days, tomorrow, in the future, next, later on, later
Importance: foremost, most importantly, especially, of less importance, of least importance
In earlier centuries there was no need for elaborate accounting systems. But the size of today's businesses makes modern accounting a complicated process indeed.

Indicating the stages in an argument or process, or the items in a series:
initially, at the outset, to begin with, first, first of all, up to now, so far, second, thus far, next, after, finally, last of all
The accounting process works in stages. First, transactions must be analyzed.

Giving a result:
as a result, consequently, accordingly, as a consequence, therefore, thus, hence, then, for that reason, thus
Generally accepted accounting principles are continually evolving. Therefore, they are able to meet the changing needs of the business world.

Summing up or restating the central point:
in sum, to sum up, to summarize, in summary, to conclude, in brief, in short, as one can see, in conclusion
In conclusion, transitions often make writing much easier to read.

Repetition of Key Words and Phrases

Effective writers use transitional expressions not only between sentences, but also between paragraphs and between major divisions of the writing project. However, to create continuity between these larger units, they may also use an additional technique—repetition of key words or phrases. The typical location for these repetitions is at the beginning of a new paragraph or section. The following outline shows the structure of a discussion on alternatives to historical cost accounting. Notice how the combination of transitional expressions and repeated key phrases holds the parts of the report together. These techniques also tie the parts of the report to the central idea, which is defined in the thesis statement.

The Monetary Unit Assumption[1]

I. Introductory paragraph
    A. Attention-getting sentences
        One of the basic assumptions accountants made in the past was that money was an effective common denominator by which business enterprises could be measured and analyzed. Implicit in this assumption was the acceptance of the stable and unchanging nature of monetary units. Recently, however, the validity of this assumption has been questioned not only by academicians and theorists, but by practitioners as well.
    B. Thesis statement
        Several solutions have been developed by accountants to correct for the floating nature of the monetary unit.
II. Body
    A. Nature of the problem
        The unadjusted monetary unit system has been criticized because it distorts financial statements during periods of inflation.
    B. First solution to the problem
        1. One solution to overstating profits solely because of inflation is based on the purchasing power of the monetary unit. (This paragraph describes this solution and its advantages.)
        2. However, the general purchasing power approach has been criticized for several reasons. (The paragraph describes the disadvantages of this approach.)
    C. Second solution to the problem
        1. Instead of the general purchasing power procedure, the SEC favors the alternative solution of current value accounting. (Paragraph describes this solution.)
        2. One of the major advantages of the current value approach . . . (Paragraph discusses several advantages.)
        3. One authority has summarized the criticisms of current value accounting: "Most of the criticisms . . . ." (Paragraph discusses the disadvantages of this approach.)
III. Concluding paragraph
    The general purchasing power approach and the current value method of accounting both attempt to correct the problems of the monetary unit assumption in times of inflation.

Pronouns Used to
Achieve Coherence

The final tool that effective writers use to achieve coherent writing is the pronoun. A pronoun stands for a noun or a noun phrase that has previously been identified. The noun that the pronoun refers to is called its *antecedent.* Consider the following sentence:

> Firms usually issue their financial statements at least once a year.

In this sentence, the pronoun *their* refers to the noun *firms.* Put another way, *firms* is the antecedent of *their.*

Because pronouns refer to nouns that the writer has already used, pronouns help connect the thoughts of a paragraph. Look at how the pronouns work in this paragraph:

> The audit staff reviewed the financial statements of Tristram Industries to determine if the statements had been prepared in accordance with generally accepted accounting principles. *We* found two problems that may require us to issue a qualified opinion. First, Tristram has not been consistent in *its* treatment of contingencies. Second, *we* identified several transactions that may violate the concept of substance over form. Thus, *we* suggest a meeting with Tristram's management to discuss these issues.

Pronouns require a word of warning, however. Unless a writer is careful, the reader may not be sure what noun the pronoun refers to. Look at the problem in this sentence:

> The managers informed the accountants that they did not understand company policy.

Who doesn't understand company policy—the managers or the accountants? This sentence illustrates the problem of ambiguous pronoun reference. Chapter 6 discusses this problem, and ways to correct it, in greater detail.

Without these techniques to achieve coherence—logical order of ideas, transitional expressions, repetition of key words and phrases, and pronouns—writing will be much harder to understand. Therefore, we can add another rule to the list of effective writing skills:

1. **Analyze the purpose of the writing and the needs of the readers.**
2. **Use an outline to organize the ideas you want to present.**
3. **Write the rough draft, and then revise it to make the writing polished and correct.**
4. **Make your writing unified—all sentences should relate to the main idea, either directly or indirectly.**
5. **Use transitional expressions, repetition of key words and phrases, and pronouns to achieve coherent writing.**

NOTES

1. Steven C. Dabbs, ''The Monetary Unit Assumption'' (unpublished student paper, University of Georgia, 1978).

2. Charles T. Horngren, *Introduction to Financial Accounting* (Englewood Cliffs, N.J.: Prentice-Hall, Inc., © 1981), p. 13. Reprinted by permission.
3. Doug Hertha, "Audit Report of Charter Air" (unpublished student paper, University of Georgia, 1982).
4. Jean Bryan, "Finance and Accounting Considerations in Issuing Convertible Debt" (unpublished student paper, University of Georgia, 1980).

EXERCISES

Exercise 3-1

Peter Dowling is a junior staff accountant for a small CPA firm in Austin, Texas. The senior partners have asked him to investigate two computer systems for possible purchase by the firm. The partners have also asked him to recommend the system that the firm should buy. Peter has drafted the following outline for his report and asked for your critique.

   I. Introduction
  II. The history of computer technology
 III. Simple Sam Computer Model B-13
      A. General description of features
      B. Nearest service center in Dallas, Texas
      C. Can handle much of firm's computer work
      D. Limited capacity for future expansion
      E. Takes up only a small amount of office space
 IV. Whiz Kid Computer Model 1004
      A Easily adaptable in the future to new programs and functions
      B. Slightly larger than the Simple Sam Model
      C. Service center in Austin
      D. Can handle all the firm's current computer work
      E. General description of features
  V. The need for accountants to have more training in computer science
 VI. The role of computers in the future of accounting
VII. Conclusion

1. What is the purpose of Peter's report?
2. What do you think is the main idea of the report?
3. What material included in Peter's outline is irrelevant to his purpose?
4. What necessary information has he forgotten to include?
5. Are the ideas in the outline arranged logically? If not, rearrange the ideas into a more effective outline. Include only relevant material.
6. What kinds of transitional devices could Peter use when he writes his report? Rewrite the outline in sentence form, and include transitional devices.

Exercise 3-2

Identify the transitional devices (transitional expressions, repetition of key words and phrases, pronouns) in the following paragraphs. Note how logically these devices tie the sentences together.

1. (1) Under the FIFO method, ending inventory will consist of the last units purchased. (2) Accountants often favor this method of accounting for inventories because it is easier to apply and more logical than some of the other methods. (3) FIFO also gives a more accurate inventory estimate on the balance sheet. (4) However, FIFO does not give an accurate picture of earnings during times of inflation.

2. (1) The specific identification method of inventory accounting is usually more time-consuming and costly than other methods. (2) Also, a business could use this method to manipulate earnings by recording the lowest possible price for a particular item sold and thus increase earnings on that item. (3) Because of these problems, few businesses use specific identification.

3. (1) The vast bulk of purchases (and sales) throughout the world are conducted on a *credit* basis rather than on a *cash* basis. (2) This "buy now, pay later" attitude is particularly prevalent in dealings among manufacturers, wholesalers, and retailers. (3) Indeed, the extension of credit seems to be a major lubricant of the world's economies. (4) Thus, unless a customer is considered a dangerous credit risk, cash is not expected until a later date. (5) Furthermore, an "authorized signature" of the buyer is usually sufficient; no formal promissory note is necessary. (6) This practice is known as buying (or selling) on open account; the debt is shown on the buyer's balance sheet as an account payable.[2]

Exercise 3-3

Some of the following paragraphs are effectively organized, but some lack unity and/or coherence. Analyze the paragraphs to decide which ones need revision. Then revise the faulty paragraphs, using some of these techniques:

- a strong topic sentence stating the paragraph's main idea
- transitional devices showing the relation between sentences
- elimination of sentences that don't fit
- division of long, ununified paragraphs into shorter, unified ones
- rearranging sentences by grouping relevant ideas together (add sentences if necessary)

1. Government accountants help national, state, and local governments control spending and budgeting. Government spending could run rampant. Governmental accounting is similar to industrial accounting in many of its functions. Government accountants prevent the government from wasting taxpayers' money.

2. One service that public accountants perform is auditing. Accountants examine clients' financial statements to see if they are in conformity with Generally Accepted Accounting Principles. Accountants give credibility to financial statements. Public accountants offer management advisory services. Management consultants suggest ways firms can improve such functions as information processing, budgeting, and accounting systems. Taxes are an increasingly complex area. Accountants prepare and file returns and advise clients how to incur the smallest tax liability on a transaction.

3. The controversy centers on several financial statement adjustments that the audit staff has proposed. First, legal fees of $100,000 incurred in obtaining an exclusive route in a resort area had been deferred to future periods. Charter Air Corporation obtained the

route in 1976, but dropped it in early 1979 due to insufficient travel. Second, $150,000 in fees and expenses relating to an air freight agreement with a local manufacturer were also deferred. However, the manufacturer felt that the service was too costly and has since discontinued its use. Because neither of these deferrals is of any future benefit, we recommend that Charter write both off in 1979. Finally, the audit staff proposes an obsolescence reserve of approximately $250,000 in the spare parts inventory. All together, these three adjustments would add $500,000 to the 1979 loss and would make the firm's already bad year look worse. Management thus opposes making the adjustments.[3]

4. Industrial accountants prepare financial reports for the firms they work for. They may prepare budget reports, tax forms, statements of earnings, balance sheets, and cost studies. Industrial accountants receive fringe benefits such as paid vacations, pensions, and insurance. In larger firms accountants may specialize in internal auditing, which sees that the company follows Generally Accepted Accounting Principles. Cost accounting deals with the costs of different phases of production of the company's products. A tax accountant files tax forms and tries to minimize the company's tax liability. A budget specialist may draft new budgets or examine expenditures to see that they conform with budgets already adopted. Industrial accountants often advance to top positions in their firms. The average starting salary is about $15,000.

5. Many corporations can benefit from convertible debt. Firms should be aware of the hardships that may arise from conversion or nonconversion. Firms should be aware that accounting requirements impose a potentially unfavorable presentation of debt in the financial statements. Corporations want to obtain low-cost funds now, and desire also to increase their equity in the future.

6. Although the purchase of our supplier's stock may offer us several advantages, there are also some potential problems we should consider. For one thing, we may not always need the supplier's raw material, because we may not always manufacture the product that requires this material. And even if we continue to manufacture our product, our research and development staff may develop a cheaper, synthetic raw material. Finally, if we do purchase the stock but later need to resell it, we cannot be assured that the stock will be marketable at that time.

Exercise 3-4

Write a sentence outline for one of the following topics. Assume the outline is for a 500–1,000 word report that you are preparing for your client, Alfred O'Neil. Alfred is the owner/manager of a small hardware store with ten employees. He is astute about business matters, but he has little training in accounting.

Include in your outline a sentence stating the main idea or purpose of the report. Divide your subject into logical subtopics, stating in a sentence the main idea of each division. Finally, show the transition devices you would use to tie the report together. (For a model outline, see p. 19 of this chapter.)

Topics:

1. How to reconcile a bank statement.
2. Internal control for cash in Alfred O'Neil's store. (You may want to narrow this topic to one aspect of internal control, such as control over the cash registers.)
3. Possible causes for low inventory turnover in the store's home remodeling department. (Invent some possible causes for this hypothetical situation.)

ANSWERS TO EXERCISES

Answers, Exercise 3-1

1. The purpose of Peter's report is to compare the two computer systems and to recommend the better system for his firm.

2. The report's main idea might be stated like this:
   Because of its several advantages—adaptability to future use, versatility for present use, convenient location of the service center—the Whiz Kid system would be the wiser purchase.

3. Outline sections II, V, and VI are irrelevant to the report's purpose. The history of computer technology, the need for accountants to have more computer training, and the role of computers in the future of accounting will not affect the choice of computer systems for Peter's firm.

4. Answers to this question will vary. Perhaps most obviously, Peter has forgotten to include the systems' costs in his outline.

5. Here is one possible outline for Peter's report:

   I. Introduction, including the main idea
   II. Simple Sam Model B-13
       A. General description of features
       B. Costs
       C. Advantage: takes up only a small amount of office space
       D. Disadvantages
           1. Nearest service center is in Dallas, Texas
           2. Cannot handle all of firm's computer work
           3. Limited capacity for future expansion
   III. Whiz Kid Model 1004
       A. General description
       B. Costs
       C. Advantages
           1. Easily adaptable in the future to new programs
           2. Service center is in Austin
           3. Can handle all the firm's current computer work
       D. Disadvantage: slightly larger than the Simple Sam Model.
   IV. Conclusion

6. Peter could expand the outline to indicate transitional devices:

   I. Introduction
   Main idea: Because of its several advantages—adaptability to future use, versatility for present use, convenient location of service center—the Whiz Kid system would be the wiser purchase.
   II. One system that might be suitable for our firm is the Simple Sam Model B-13.
       A. This model has a number of features that make it suitable for a firm such as ours. For example, . . .
       B. The Simple Sam computer is relatively inexpensive to purchase and operate.
       C. The model offers one important advantage for our company: it would take up only a small amount of office space.
       D. However, the Simple Sam System has a number of disadvantages that may limit it for our purposes. For one thing, . . .

III. A computer system that may be preferable for our firm is the Whiz Kid Model 1004.
   A. This computer offers most of the same features as the Simple Sam model and some additional features that give it added versatility.
   B. The costs of the Whiz Kid are comparable to those of Simple Sam.
   C. This computer will offer several important advantages for our firm. First, . . .
   D. Although the Whiz Kid offers all of these attractive features, it does have one drawback.
IV. Conclusion
   Thus, in spite of the additional office space it will require, I recommend the Whiz Kid because of its many advantages for our firm.

Answers, Exercise 3-2

1. (2) it—pronoun
        method/methods, inventories—repetition of key words
   (3) FIFO, inventory—repetition of key words
        also—transitional expression
   (4) FIFO—repetition of key word
        however—transitional expression
2. (2) method—repetition of key word
        also—transitional expression
   (3) specific identification—repetition of key phrase
3. (3) credit—repetition of key word
        indeed—transitional expression
   (4) credit, cash—repetition of key words
        thus—transitional expression
   (5) furthermore—transitional expression
   (6) buyer—repetition of key word

Answers, Exercise 3-3

1. This paragraph needs revision. Here is one possibility:

   Government accountants help national, state, and local governments control spending and budgeting. Without controls, government spending could run rampant. Thus, one function of government accountants is to prevent the government from wasting taxpayers' money.

2. This paragraph also needs revision:

   Public accountants offer a variety of services to the public. One such service is auditing. An auditor examines a client's financial statements to see if they are fair and prepared in conformity with Generally Accepted Accounting Principles. Accountants thus give credibility to a firm's financial statements. Another service that the public accountant offers is management advisory services. Management consultants suggest ways firms can improve such functions as information processing, budgeting, and accounting systems. Finally, public accountants may aid the public in the increasingly complex area of taxes. Tax accountants prepare and file tax returns and advise clients how to incur the smallest tax liability on a transaction.

3. This paragraph, though complex and technical, is unified and coherent. Note the effective use of transitional devices.

4. This long paragraph should be divided into several shorter ones. In addition, some of the sentences need rearranging into a more logical order.

> Industrial accountants prepare financial reports for the firms they work for. For example, they may prepare budget reports, tax forms, statements of earnings, balance sheets, and cost studies.
>
> In large firms industrial accountants may specialize in a certain kind of accounting service. Internal auditors, for example, see that the company follows Generally Accepted Accounting Principles. Cost accountants help analyze and control the costs of producing the company's products. A specialist in tax files tax forms and tries to minimize the company's tax liability. Finally, a budget specialist drafts new budgets and analyzes the effectiveness of budgets already adopted.
>
> Industrial accounting offers many opportunities. Although starting salaries average only around $15,000, promotions and salary increases usually come quickly to competent employees. In addition to their salaries, industrial accountants also receive fringe benefits such as paid vacations, pensions, and insurance.

5. This paragraph also needs revision. One possibility:

> Many corporations can benefit from convertible debt, especially corporations that want to obtain low-cost funds now, and desire also to increase their equity in the future. However, firms considering convertible debt financing should be aware of the hardships that may arise from conversion or from nonconversion; they should also be aware that accounting requirements impose a potentially unfavorable presentation of such debt in the financial statements.[4]

6. This paragraph is acceptable as it is written.

Chapter 4

PARAGRAPHS: THE BASIC UNIT OF ALL WRITING

Accountants may write anything, from memos of one paragraph to reports of many pages. The basic unit of all their writing, whatever the length, is the paragraph. Well-structured, well-developed paragraphs go a long way toward achieving effective writing.

LENGTH

Inexperienced writers are not always sure how long paragraphs should be. Are one-sentence paragraphs acceptable? What about paragraphs that run on for nearly an entire typed page?

One rule is that a paragraph should be limited to the development of one idea. Thus, the length of most paragraphs is somewhere between one sentence and an entire page. However, an occasional short paragraph, even of only one sentence, may be effective to emphasize an idea or to provide a transition between two major divisions of the writing.

Effective writers, remembering the needs of their readers, will be wary of paragraphs much longer than half a page. Very long paragraphs look intimidating, and are often hard to follow. You may need to divide a long paragraph into two shorter ones. Appropriate transitions can tie the two paragraphs together and maintain a smooth flow of thought.

STRUCTURE

Another feature of well-written paragraphs is their structure. Chapter 3 discussed how a strong topic sentence can contribute to a unified paragraph. A topic sentence states the main idea of the paragraph. It is usually the first sentence in the paragraph, and sometimes it contains a transition tying the new paragraph to the previous one. All other sentences in the paragraph should develop the idea expressed in the topic sentence.

Two patterns of paragraph organization are useful for accountants' writing tasks—the simple-deductive paragraph and the complex-deductive paragraph. The simple-deductive arrangement states the main idea in the first sentence (topic sentence); all other sentences *directly* develop that idea through explanation, illustration, or analysis. A concluding sentence is optional. Here is an example of a simple-deductive paragraph.

> (1) Accountants never finish their educations. (2) They work hard for their college degrees, but after college they must continue studying to stay current on the latest developments in the profession. (3) They must be thoroughly familiar with changing governmental regulations and new pronouncements by professional organizations like the FASB. (4) To improve their professional competence, they participate in a variety of continuing education programs sponsored by such organizations as the AICPA and state accounting societies. (5) Indeed, well-qualified accountants will be lifetime students, always seeking better ways to serve their clients and the public.

In this paragraph, sentence 1 is the topic sentence, sentences 2–4 develop the main idea, and sentence 5 is the conclusion. A simple-deductive paragraph has a simple structural diagram:

(1) Topic sentence—main idea
    (2) Supporting sentence
    (3) Supporting sentence
    (4) Supporting sentence
(5) Concluding sentence (optional)

A complex-deductive paragraph has a more elaborate structure. The paragraph analyzed first in Chapter 3 is complex-deductive:

> (1) Financial statements are important to a variety of users. (2) First, investors and potential investors use the statements to decide if a company is a good investment risk. (3) These users look at such factors as net income, the debt-to-equity ratio, and retained earnings. (4) Second, creditors use financial statements to decide if a firm is a good credit risk. (5) Creditors want to know if a firm has a large enough cash flow to pay its debts. (6) Third, governmental agencies analyze financial statements for a variety of purposes. (7) For example, the Internal Revenue Service will want to know

if the company has paid the required amount of taxes on its income. (8) These examples of financial statement users show how diverse their interests can be.

In this paragraph, sentence 1 (topic sentence) states the main idea. Sentence 2 directly supports the main idea by giving an example of it, but sentence 3 explains sentence 2. Thus sentence 3 directly supports sentence 2, but only indirectly supports sentence 1. Complex-deductive paragraphs have a structural diagram similar to this one:

(1) Topic sentence—main idea
    (2) Direct support
        (3) Indirect support
    (4) Direct support
        (5) Indirect support
    (6) Direct support
        (7) Indirect support
(8) Conclusion

Complex-deductive paragraphs can have numerous variations. The number of direct supporting sentences can vary, as can the number of indirect supports. Sometimes direct supports may not require any indirect supports.

Consider another example of a complex-deductive paragraph:

(1) Two of the most popular inventory flow assumptions used by businesses today are FIFO (first-in, first-out) and LIFO (last-in, first-out). (2) FIFO assumes that the first goods purchased for inventory are the first goods sold. (3) Therefore, ending inventory under FIFO consists of the most recent purchases. (4) Because older, usually lower costs are matched with sales revenues, FIFO results in a higher net income and thus higher income tax liabilities. (5) The LIFO flow assumption, on the other hand, assumes that the most recent purchases are the first goods sold. (6) Ending inventory under LIFO will consist of older, usually less expensive goods. (7) Cost of goods sold, however, will be based on more recent, higher prices. (8) Thus LIFO usually results in lower net income and lower income tax liabilities. (9) This advantage makes LIFO very popular with many businesses.

This paragraph can be outlined to reveal the following structure:

I. Topic sentence (1): Two popular inventory flow assumptions
    A. FIFO (2–4)
        1. description (2)
        2. effect on inventory (3)
        3. effect on net income and taxes (4)
    B. LIFO (5–9)
        1. description (5)
        2. effect on inventory (6)
        3. effect on net income and taxes (7–8)
        4. popularity (9)

The descriptions of FIFO and LIFO in this paragraph are, of course, very condensed—probably too condensed for most purposes. The paragraph could be expanded into a longer discussion with more detailed explanations and examples, but the complex-deductive structure would still be a good pattern of organization.

The important idea about both simple- and complex-deductive paragraphs is their unity; all sentences, either directly or indirectly, develop the main idea of the paragraph as expressed in the topic sentence.

Some writers may wonder about a third type of paragraph organization— paragraphs with an inductive arrangement of ideas. Inductive paragraphs put the main idea last; supporting sentences lead up to the topic sentence, which is, of course, the last sentence in the paragraph.

For most business writing, inductive paragraphs are not as effective as a simple- or complex-deductive organization. Business readers like to identify main ideas from the start; they don't like to be kept in suspense, wondering "What's all this leading up to? What's the point?" So it's a good idea to stick with deductive organization for most, if not all, of your paragraphs.

The final point about paragraph structure is a reminder about the need for transitions to tie the sentences of the paragraph together. Chapter 3 showed how transitions create a smooth flow of ideas without abrupt jumps in the thought process. However, transitions, especially transitional expressions, can be over-used. Frequently, the connection between sentences is obvious from their meaning, and then transitional expressions are superfluous. Read again the paragraph on page 28. This paragraph is easy to follow, but it doesn't use a single transitional expression.

PARAGRAPH DEVELOPMENT

An effective paragraph is not only well organized; it is also well developed. That is, the idea expressed in the topic sentence is adequately explained and illustrated so that the reader has a clear understanding of what the writer wishes to say.

Several techniques are useful for paragraph development: illustrations or ex- amples, definitions, descriptive and factual details, and appeals to authority.

Probably the most useful technique of paragraph development is illustrations or examples—typical cases or specific instances of the idea being discussed. Il- lustrations can take a variety of forms. Sometimes a paragraph will combine several brief examples, or it may use one long, extended illustration. The examples may be factually true, or they may be hypothetical—invented for the purpose of illustration. A good writer will often combine illustrations with other techniques of paragraph development.

Definitions are particularly useful to explain concepts or terms which might be unfamiliar to the reader. A definition can be formal, such as the meaning given in a dictionary or accounting textbook, or it can be a more informal explanation of a term. Frequently a definition is more effective when combined with an illustration. Here is a paragraph developed by definition and illustration:

> *Assets* can be defined as "things possessing service potential or utility to their owner that can be measured and expressed in money terms."[1] For example, cash is an asset; so are the land, buildings, and equipment owned by a business. Sometimes assets are resources legally owned by a business, though not tangible. An example of this kind of asset is an account receivable.

Descriptive and factual details give a more thorough, concrete explanation of the idea expressed in a general way in the topic sentence. Factual details give measurable, observable, or historical information that can be objectively verified. Descriptive details are similar to factual details; they give specific characteristics of the subject being discussed.

The following paragraph combines definition, detail, and illustration.

> The matching principle relates revenues generated during a period with the expenses required to produce those revenues. Thus revenues earned from sales are matched with such expenses as production costs, advertising, and sales commissions. Accurately matching expenses with revenues results in a truer picture of a business's profitability during a given period of time.

Finally, some paragraphs are developed by appeals to authority—facts, illustrations, or ideas obtained from a reputable source such as a book, article, interview, or official pronouncement. Appeals to authority may be paraphrases—someone else's idea expressed in your own words—or direct quotations from the source being used. The paragraph at the top of this page uses a direct quotation from an accounting textbook to provide an authoritative definition of *assets*. Chapter 6 gives more information on the correct use of quotations and paraphrases.

By using a variety of techniques, then, effective writers fully develop the ideas expressed in the topic sentences of their paragraphs. Illustration, definition, factual and descriptive detail, and authority—all of these techniques give the reader a clear understanding of what the writer wishes to explain.

This chapter has discussed the sixth and seventh rules for good writing.

1. **Analyze the purpose of the writing and the needs of the readers.**
2. **Use an outline to organize the ideas you want to present.**
3. **Write the rough draft, and then revise it to make the writing polished and correct.**
4. **Unify the writing—all sentences should relate to the main idea, either directly or indirectly.**
5. **Use transitional expressions, repetition of key words and phrases, and pronouns to achieve coherent writing.**
6. **Organize paragraphs by either a simple-deductive or a complex-deductive arrangement of supporting sentences.**
7. **Develop paragraphs by illustration, definition, detail, and appeals to authority.**

NOTES

1. James Don Edwards, Roger H. Hermanson, and R. F. Salmonson, *Financial Accounting: A Programmed Text,* 4th ed. (Homewood, Ill.: Richard D. Irwin, Inc., 1978), p. 33.
2. Allan Bashinski, "Accounting Careers" (unpublished student paper, University of Georgia, 1982).
3. Adapted from Charles T. Horngren, *Introduction to Financial Accounting* (Englewood Cliffs, N.J.: Prentice-Hall, Inc., © 1981), p. 6. Reprinted by permission.
4. Charles T. Horngren, *Introduction to Management Accounting,* 5th ed. (Englewood Cliffs, N.J.: Prentice-Hall, Inc., © 1981), p. 5. Reprinted by permission.
5. Greg Thompson, "Land Option Costs" (unpublished student paper, University of Georgia, 1982).

EXERCISES

Exercise 4-1

For the following paragraphs, identify

- Structure (simple-deductive, complex-deductive)
- Major and minor supports in complex-deductive paragraphs
- Transitional devices
- Techniques of development (single or multiple examples, definition, factual and/or descriptive detail, appeal to authority, or a combination of techniques)

1. (1) One career alternative for accounting graduates is with the government. (2) Government accountants oversee the financial records of federal, state, and local agencies. (3) They also examine the records of individuals and businesses that are subject to government regulations. (4) The Internal Revenue Service, for example, assumes these tasks as a public service. (5) Performing services similar to management accountants, government accountants also budget administrative costs and plans for future operations, record transactions and events, prepare financial statements, and electronically process accounting data for government bureaucracies.[2]

2. (1) The accounting profession may be classified in many ways; a major classification is public accounting and private accounting. (2) "Public" accountants are those whose services are rendered to the general public on a fee basis. (3) Such services include auditing, income taxes, and management consulting. (4) "Private" accountants are all the rest. (5) They consist of not only those individuals who work for businesses but also those who work for government agencies, including the Internal Revenue Service.[3]

3. (1) The audit staff reviewed Brockwood Corporation's revenue cycles to understand the stystem controls. (2) Our review included order processing, sales invoicing, and accounts receivable. (3) We performed procedural tests to confirm our flowchart documentation of the system. (4) We also reviewed the revenue cycle accounting entries for the December 31 accounts receivable balances.

4. (1) The audit staff found several problems with Gigantic's accounts receivable. (2) For example, corporate policy for recording the sale of obsolete inventory is to reduce the reserve and inventory by the amount established for obsolete inventory. (3) Gigantic then recognizes the amount of sales as income. (4) Last February, the company sold three terminals to Underwood, Inc., for $20,300. (5) Gigantic's accountant then reduced the inventory reserve for the difference between the established allowance of $45,600 and the sales price of $20,300. (6) As a result, the inventory reserve is overstated by $20,300, and the receivables are understated by $20,300.

5. (1) An accounting system is a formal means of gathering data to aid and coordinate collective decisions in light of the overall goals or objectives of an organization. (2) The accounting system is the major quantitative information system in almost every organization. (3) An effective accounting system provides information for three broad purposes or ends: internal reporting to managers, for use in planning and controlling routine operations; internal reporting to managers, for use in strategic planning—that is, the making of special decisions and the formulating of overall policies and long-range plans; and external reporting to stockholders, government, and other outside parties.[4]

6. (1) Purchase options on land represent payments to the owners of property giving one the right during a specified period to buy a site or pass up the purchase opportunity. (2) Accounting for these options presents problems for today's accountant. (3) He must decide whether to capitalize the cost of the option in a land account or to expense the cost in the immediate period. (4) Further complications exist when clients acquire several options on suitable sites with intentions of choosing the best alternative. (5) Here, the accountant must consider several factors before recording the costs incurred, including materiality and future expectations.[5]

Exercise 4-2: Writing Topics

Discuss the following topics in well-organized and well-developed paragraphs. Remember the techniques for effective paragraphs covered in this and previous chapters: unity, coherence, length, structure, and development.

1. Conservatism
2. Foreign Corrupt Practices Act
3. Internal control
4. Reversing entries
5. Stockholders' equity
6. Cash
7. Responsibility accounting
8. Capitalization
9. Cost center
10. Direct labor
11. FASB
12. GAAP
13. Tax deferral
14. Double entries

ANSWERS TO EXERCISES

Answers, Exercise 4-1

1. • Structure: complex-deductive
    • Supports:
    (2),(4)—major
    (1)—minor
    • Transitional devices:
    (2)   government—repetition of key word
    (3)   they—pronoun
          also—transitional expression
          government—repetition of key word
    (4)   for example—transitional expression
    (5)   government accountants—repetition of key phrase
          also—transitional expression
          government—repetition of key word
    • Techniques of development:
       detail, example
2. • Structure: complex-deductive
    • Supports:
    (2),(4)—major
    (3),(5)—minor
    • Transitional devices:
    (2)   public—repetition of key word
    (3)   services—repetition of key word
    (4)   private, accountants—repetition of key words
    (5)   they—pronoun
    • Techniques of development:
       detail, examples
3. • Structure: simple-deductive
    • Transitional devices:
    (2)   our—pronoun
          review—repetition of key word (variant of ''reviewed'' in (1))
    (3)   we—pronoun
          system—repetition of key word
    (4)   also—transitional expression
          reviewed, revenue cycle—repetition of key word and phrase
    • Technique of development: detail
4. • Structure: simple-deductive
    • Transitional devices:
    (2)   for example—transitional expression
    (3)   Gigantic—repetition of key word
          then—transitional expression
          sales—repetition of key word
    (5)   Gigantic's—repetition of key word
          inventory reserve—repetition of key phrase
    (6)   As a result—transitional expression
          inventory reserve, receivables—repetition of key phrase and word

5. • Structure: simple-deductive
    • Transitional devices:
        (2)   accounting system—repetition of key phrase
        (3)   accounting system—repetition of key phrase
    • Techniques of development:
        definition, details

6. • Structure and supports: The structure of this paragraph is not easy to analyze. The topic sentence is the second sentence; sentence (1) is a supporting sentence—a definition.

    We might decide that this paragraph is simple-deductive, although some people would argue that it is complex. As a complex-deductive paragraph, it would have the following structure:
        (1)   major support
        (2)   topic sentence
        (3),(4)   major supports
        (5)   minor support
    • Transitional devices:
        (2)   options—repetition of key word
        (3)   he—pronoun
        (4)   further—transitional expression
              options—repetition of key word
        (5)   here—transitional expression
    • Techniques of development:
        definition, details

Chapter 5

STYLE

An effective writing style is interesting and easy to read. Poor writing is almost everywhere—in textbooks, scholarly journals, government publications, and even in official pronouncements of the accounting profession. Indeed, sometimes it seems that accountants have more poor writing models than good ones.

If you wish to develop effective writing, it is important that you develop a clear, vivid writing style. Textbooks on writing often give long lists of suggestions to help writers improve their style. To keep our writing process as simple as possible, however, this handbook suggests only six techniques for good style. If you understand and apply these techniques, you will notice a remarkable improvement in your writing style: writing that is clear, interesting, and easy to read.

Let's look at these techniques one at a time and see how much they can contribute to effective writing.

CONCRETION

The first suggestion will appear familiar; Chapter 4 discusses this technique as a part of good paragraph development.

Be concrete: use facts, details, and examples.

Concrete writing can be explained by defining its opposite, abstract writing. Abstract writing is vague, general, or theoretical. It is hard to understand because it is not illustrated by particular, material objects. Concrete writing, on the other hand, is vivid and specific; it brings a picture into the mind of the reader.

Illustrations of abstract and concrete writing styles will make them easier to understand.

Abstract:

Historical cost is important in accounting. It is easy for accountants to use, and it is often seen in the financial statements. Historical cost has some disadvantages, but it has its good points, too.

Concrete:

Historical cost often refers to the amount of money actually paid for an object at the time it was purchased. For example, if a truck was purchased in 1975 for $10,000, then $10,000 would be the truck's historical cost. Many accountants favor historical cost accounting because the values of assets are easy to determine from invoices and other records of the original purchase. However, in times of inflation the historical cost of an asset may not indicate its true value. For example, an acre of land bought in 1950 for $5,000 might be worth several times that amount today, but it would still be recorded in the owner's books, and the statement of financial position, at its historical cost. Thus one disadvantage of historical cost accounting is that it often undervalues assets.

By giving more detailed information and specific, concrete examples of historical cost, the second paragraph makes this concept easier to understand and more interesting to read.

ACTIVE AND PASSIVE VOICE

The second technique for achieving a good writing style may seem technical, but it too will become clear after a few definitions and examples.

Use active voice whenever possible.

First of all, we'd better define active and passive voice. Sentences are usually written in active voice. The subject of the sentence performs the action described by the verb.

ACTIVE: Most corporations issue financial statements at least once a year.

Passive voice, on the other hand, describes action done *to* somebody or something *by* another agent; the agent is not always named in the sentence.

PASSIVE: Financial statements are issued (by most corporations) at least once a year.

Students can learn to recognize passive voice by its formula:

Passive Voice = a form of the + the past participle of a verb
            verb *to be*   (usually ending in *-ed*)

TYPICAL FORMS OF THE VERB *TO*   **TYPICAL PAST PARTICIPLES:**
BE:

is, are, were, was, been, being, be   accrued, received, used, computed, given,
kept

Sometimes passive verb phrases also contain a form of *to have* (has, have, had, etc.) or an auxiliary (will, should, would, will, must, etc.), but passive voice always contains a *to be* form plus a past participle.

Active-voice sentences are usually more effective than passive-voice sentences. Consider the following examples:

PASSIVE   **ACTIVE**

Taxes *were increased* by fifty percent.   Congress *increased* taxes by fifty percent.

(In this example, most readers would want to know *who* raised taxes.)

Deliberate understatement of assets and stockholders' equity with the intention of misleading interested parties *is prohibited.*	SEC regulations *prohibit* deliberate misstatement of assets and stockholders' equity if the intention is to mislead interested parties.
Bonds *are issued* by a company when it wants to increase long-term funds without issuing additional capital stock.	A company *issues* bonds when it wants to increase long-term funds without issuing additional capital stock.

Unfortunately, writers of "officialese," especially in government, business, and research, have so badly overused passive voice that we tend to accept it as standard style. But passive voice is seldom effective—it lacks the forcefulness and clarity of active voice. Compare these sentences:

PASSIVE: The problem of keeping track of the flow of funds was simplified by use of the company's system of internal controls.
 ACTIVE: The internal control system proved effective in tracing the flow of funds.[1]

A good writer will avoid using passive voice in most situations. He will ask himself two questions. What is the action (verb)? Who or what is doing it (subject)? One writer makes sure his sentences are in active voice by asking, "Who's kicking who?"[2]

Occasionally, of course, you will need to use passive voice to avoid an awkward sentence. But use active voice whenever you can.

One word of warning: avoid substituting a weak active verb for passive voice.

Be particularly careful of colorless verbs like *to exist* and *to occur*. The following sentences are written in active voice, but the sentences are weak:

> Capitalization of option costs on land subsequently purchased should occur.
> FIFO bases itself on the assumption that the first inventory acquired is the first inventory sold.

Try to find descriptive, vigorous verbs to substitute for weak verbs or reword the sentence.

> Accountants should capitalize option costs on land subsequently purchased.
> The assumption that underlies FIFO is that the first inventory acquired is the first inventory sold.

If you can't think of a strong active verb, or if the sentence is awkward in active voice, then leave it in passive.

> Option costs on land subsequently purchased should be capitalized.
> FIFO is based on the assumption that the first inventory acquired is the first inventory sold.

SIMPLICITY

Another bad habit many business writers get into is using big words and long, complicated sentences. Such writing is hard to read. Look at the following sentence.

> An increase in an employee's rate of pay will not become effective prior to the date on which the employee has completed a minimum of 13 weeks actual work at his regular occupational classification.

If we simplify this sentence, its meaning will be easier to understand.

> An employee must work at least 13 weeks at his regular job before he can receive an increase in pay.[3]

Sometimes words and sentences get so complicated that their meaning is completely lost:

> Ultimate consumer means a person or group of persons, generally constituting a domestic household, who purchase eggs generally at the individual stores of retailers or purchase and receive deliveries of eggs at the place of abode of the individual or domestic household from producers or retail route sellers and who use such eggs for their consumption as food.

Translation:

> Ultimate consumers are people who buy eggs to eat them.[4]

Therefore, the third technique for effective writing style is simplicity: *Keep it simple—simple vocabulary and short sentences.*

A good writer will use short, everyday words as much as possible. For example, he will write *use* instead of *utilize, help* instead of *assistance.* Shorter, familiar words are easier to read and make writing more forceful.

The chart on pages 40–42 shows two columns of words. Column B lists short, familiar words; Column A lists longer, more difficult words that are often substituted for the everyday words in Column B. The chart also shows how single words ("because") can often replace phrases ("for the reason that"). As a general rule, use the words and phrases in Column B rather than those in Column A.

Another way to achieve a simple, readable style is to use short sentences. *The average sentence should be about fifteen to twenty words long.* Short sentences are particularly important when you are explaining complicated ideas.

Note that fifteen to twenty words is an *average.* Some sentences will be longer, some shorter. In fact, it is a good idea to vary sentence lengths so the writing doesn't become monotonous. Sentence variation will be discussed again under the heading "Variety and Rhythm" (see pages 44–46).

SIMPLIFYING WORD CHOICES

As a rule, use the words and phrases in Column B rather than those in Column A.

COLUMN A	COLUMN B
above-mentioned firms	these firms
absolutely essential	essential
activate	begin
advise	tell
aggregate	total
anticipate	expect
along the lines of	like
assist	help
as per your request	as you requested
at all times	always
at this point in time	now
at this time	now
attempt	try
communicate	write, tell
commence	begin
completely eliminated	eliminated
comprise	include
consider	think
constitute	are, is
disutility	uselessness

demonstrate	show
discontinue	stop
due to the fact that	because, since
during the time that	while
earliest convenience	promptly
effort	work
enclosed herewith	enclosed
enclosed please find	enclosed is
endeavor	try
exercise care	be careful
facilitate	ease, simplify
failed to	didn't
few in number	few
for the purpose of	for
for the reason that	since
from the point of view that	for
furnish	send, give
i.e.	that is
implement	carry out
in advance of	before
in many cases	often
in all cases	always
in most cases	usually
inasmuch as	since
in behalf of	for
in connection with	about
indicate	show, point out
initiate	begin
in terms of	in
in the amount of	of, for
in the case of	if
in the event that (of)	if
in the nature of	like
in the neighborhood of	about
in this case	here
investigate	study
in view of the fact that	because, since
it has come to my attention	Mr. Jones has just told me; I have just learned
it is felt	I feel; we feel
it is our understanding that	we understand that
it should be noted that	omit
maintain	keep
maintain cost control	control cost
make application to	apply
make contact with	see, meet
make a purchase	buy
maximum	most, largest
minimum	least, smallest
modification	change
obtain	get
on the order of	about
on the part of	by

optimum	best
past history	history
per annum	annually, per year
period of time	time, period
pertaining to	about, for
philosophy	plan, idea
please be advised that	omit
please don't hestiate to call on us	please write us
prepare a job analysis	analyze a job
presently	now
prior to	before
procure	get, buy
provide continuous indication	indicate continuously
provide	give
pursuant to your inquiry	as you requested
range all the way from	range from
regarding	about
relative to	about
represent	be, is, are
require	need
so as to	to
subsequent to	after, later
substantial	large, big
sufficient	enough
terminate	end, stop
the major part of	most of
the manner in which	how
the undersigned; the writer	I, me
through the use of	by, with
true facts	facts
thereon, thereof, thereto, therefrom	omit
this is to acknowledge	thank you for
this is to inform you that we shall send	we'll send
transpire	happen
under separate cover	by June 1, tomorrow, separately, by parcel post
until such time as	until
utilize	use
vital	important
with a view to	to
with reference to	about
with regard to	about
with respect to	on, for, of, about
with the object to	to
with the result that	so that

CONCISENESS

Good writing is not only simple; it is also concise. That is, it contains no unnecessary elements—no extra words, phrases, sentences, or paragraphs.

Be concise—make every word count.

Usually, writing that is written simply is also concise. Thus, many of the techniques just discussed (see the section on "Simplicity") also reduce the number of words in a sentence without sacrificing meaning.

To make your writing concise, first check the list of words and expressions on pp. 40–42. Use single words rather than phrases whenever possible.

Next, go through your writing and see how many words can be crossed out, often with only a simple revision of the sentence. Beware of dead words—words that fill up space wihtout adding meaning. Here are some examples of sentences littered (and padded) with dead words:

WORDY: *There are* several advantages to current value accounting. (8 words)
CONCISE: Current value accounting offers several advantages. (6 words)
WORDY: *There is one organization that* has been very influential in improving the profession *of* accounting—the AICPA. (17 words)
CONCISE: The AICPA has been influential in improving the accounting profession. (10 words)

Watch out for "there is" and "there are." They can usually be eliminated. Other possibilities:[5]

WORDY	CONCISE
the question as to whether	whether
there is no doubt but that	no doubt
used for production purposes	used for production
he is a man who	he
in a hasty manner	hastily
this is a method that	this method
the reason why is that	because

"The fact that," "which is," and "which are" can usually be eliminated:

WORDY: I would like to call your attention to the fact that our earnings last month were down fifty percent. (19 words)
CONCISE: Remember that our profits were down fifty percent last month. (10 words)
                          or (even better)
          Our profits dropped fifty percent last month. (7 words)
WORDY: In spite of the fact that our costs rose by ten percent, we still were able to keep our prices stable. (21 words)
CONCISE: Although costs rose by ten percent, our prices remained stable. (10 words)
WORDY: His partner, who is an engineer, . . .
CONCISE: His partner, an engineer, . . .

Another technique to make writing more concise is to use active verbs and descriptive nouns, rather than lots of adverbs and adjectives.

WORDY: There are some serious, unfortunate results of accounting based on historical cost during times of decreasing purchasing power of the monetary unit. (22 words)

CONCISE: Historical cost accounting creates problems during periods of inflation. (9 words)

One frequent cause of wordy writing is hidden verbs. For example,

> causes a misstatement of
> *instead of*
> misstates
> provides a matching of
> *instead of*
> matches
> makes an analysis of
> *instead of*
> analyzes

What are the hidden verbs in these sentences?

> We should not make reference to any prior years' financial statements in our report.
> The company's history of marginal performance over the past several years may be an indication of future solvency problems.

In the first sentence; the hidden verb is *refer;* in the second sentence it is *indicate.* The revised sentences are a little less wordy, a little more forceful:

> We should not refer to any prior years' financial statements in our report.
> The company's history of marginal performance over the past several years may be an indication of future solvency problems.

Finally, avoid sentence introductions which weaken the sentence idea. Don't apologize or over-qualify what you say:

WORDY: This report is an attempt to explain the proper accounting treatment for loss contingencies. (14 words)
CONCISE: This report explains accounting for loss contingencies. (7 words)

In summary, clear, readable writing contains no unnecessary or dead words. Be concise—your writing will gain in forcefulness and clarity.

VARIETY AND RHYTHM

The fifth technique for an effective writing style is variety:

Vary vocabulary, sentence lengths, and sentence structures.
Read the writing aloud to hear how it sounds.

The purpose of sentence variety is to avoid monotony—a sing-song, endless repetition of the same sentence rhythms, or overuse of a word or phrase. Read the following paragraph aloud.

Financial analysts use ratios to analyze financial statements. Ratios show a company's liquidity. The current ratio shows the ratio of current assets to current liabilities. Ratios also show a company's solvency. The equity ratio is an example of a solvency ratio. It shows the ratio of owners' equity to total assets. Ratios also show profitability. The return-on-investment ratio is an example. It shows the ratio of net earnings to owners' equity.

This paragraph doesn't sound pleasing. In fact, it could easily lull the reader to sleep. The sentences are too similar in length and structure, and the word *ratio* is repeated too often. Let's try again.

Ratios based on financial statements can reveal valuable information about a company to investors, creditors, and other interested parties. Liquidity ratios show whether a company can pay its debts. The quick ratio, for example, is a good indication of debt-paying ability for companies with slow inventory turnovers. Ratios can also indicate a company's solvency; the equity ratio, for instance, shows the percentage of owners' equity to total assets. Investors use this figure to evaluate the safety of a potential investment. Finally, ratios can give a measure of a company's profitability, which is of special interest to potential investors. The earnings-per-share ratio is probably the most popular of the profitability ratios.

Another cause of monotonous sentences is too many prepositional phrases, particularly when they are linked together to form a chain. Look again at the sentence below. Prepositions are circled; the rest of the phrase is underlined.

There are some serious, unfortunate results (of) accounting based (on) historical cost (during) times (of) decreasing purchasing power (of) the monetary unit.

This sentence contains a chain of prepositional phrases five links (phrases) long. A good rule is to avoid more than two prepositional phrases in a row.

If you're not sure what prepositions are, here is a partial list:

across, after, as, at, because of, before, between, by, for, from, in, in front of, in regard to, like, near, of, on, over, through, to, together with, under, until, up, with

Variety is an important element of readable writing because it gives sentences and paragraphs a pleasing rhythm. Read your paragraphs aloud. If you notice a word or phrase repeated too often, look for a synonym. If the sentences sound choppy and monotonous, vary their structures and lengths. Often, a change in the way sentences begin will add a better rhythm to the paragraph. Add an occasional short sentence, and an occasional longer one (but be sure longer sentences are still easy to understand). And be careful of too many prepositional phrases. You don't want to bore your reader, and varied sentences are one way to keep your writing lively.

A TEST FOR READABILITY— THE FOG INDEX

Writing that is more complicated than it needs to be is sometimes called foggy writing. The ideas are obscured by unnecessary or difficult words and long, complex sentences. You can determine how foggy your writing is by a simple quantitative test called the Fog Index.[6]

Explanation of Fog Index

1. Select a sample passage of 100 to 125 words. Determine the average number of words per sentence. Treat independent clauses as separate sentences. For example, "We read. We learned. We improved." This statement should be counted as three sentences, even if semicolons or dashes are used instead of periods.
2. Determine the percentage of words on the page longer than two syllables by dividing the number of these words by the number of words in the passage. Omit from this count: (a) all capitalized words; (b) combinations of short easy words like "manpower" or "nevertheless;" and (c) verbs made into three syllables by adding "-es" or "-ed." Examples: "created" or "trespasses."
3. Add the average sentence length to the percentage of big words. Multiply the total by 0.4 to determine your Fog Index. Because few readers have more than 17 years of schooling, any passage that tests higher than 17 is given a score of "17-plus."

The Fog Index approximates the level of education needed to read any passage with ease. If the Fog Index is 13, your reader may need at least one year of college (a total of 13 years of schooling) to understand it without deep concentration. Writing with a relatively low Fog Index can communicate complex ideas. The *Wall Street Journal,* for example, has a Fog Index (readability level) averaging 11.[7]

An example will demonstrate how to compute the Fog Index. Let's analyze the following paragraph (italicized words are long words as defined in Paragraph 2 above):

> Financial statements are *important* to a *variety* of users. First, *investors* and *potential investors* use the statements to decide if a *company* is a good *investment* risk. These users look at such factors as net income, the debt-to-equity ratio, and retained earnings. Second, *creditors* use *financial* statements to decide if a firm is a good credit risk. Creditors want to know it if a firm has a large enough cash flow to pay its debts. Third, *governmental agencies analyze financial* statements for a *variety* of *purposes.* For example, the Internal Revenue Service will want to know if the *company* has paid the required amount of taxes on its income. These *examples* of *financial* statement users show how diverse their *interests* can be.

Step one. Determine the average number of words per sentence. This passage has 123 words and eight sentences. Thus the average number of words per sentence is 15.375, rounded off to 15.

Step two. Determine the percentage of the words that are longer than two syllables. Remember—*don't count*

• Capitalized words;
• Combinations of short easy words like "manpower" or "nevertheless"
• Verbs made into three syllables by adding "-es" or "-ed."

This passage has 20 of the italicized long words. Divide 20 by the 123 words in the passage for a percentage of 16.260, rounded off to 16.

Step three. Add the average sentence length and the percentage of big words, and multiply the total by 0.4:

$$
\begin{array}{ll}
15 & \text{Average sentence length} \\
\underline{16} & \text{Percentage of long words} \\
31 & \\
\underline{\times 0.4} & \\
12.4 & \text{FOG INDEX (drop digits following the decimal point)}
\end{array}
$$

Thus 12 is the Fog Index of the passage. A reader with a high school education (12 years of schooling) should have no difficulty understanding this discussion of financial statement users.

Write simply; keep fog to a minimum. Don't let your ideas be hidden by dense words and sentences.

PRECISE MEANING

Effective writing is not only interesting and easy to read; it is also precise. That is, meanings are clear and yield only one possible interpretation. Precision is particularly important in accountants' writing, because accountants are often legally responsible for the accuracy of what they write. Moreoever, the technical nature of accounting makes precise writing a necessity. The final rule for an effective writing style is, thus, precision:

Be precise—avoid ambiguous and confused meanings.

Imprecise writing can result from several causes. One culprit is poor diction, or the inaccurate use of words:

The major *setback* of the current method is verifiability.
(Poor diction. The writer meant *drawback*.)
The advantage of measurements in terms of replacement costs is that the costs reflect *what the item is worth*.
(What is the precise meaning of the italicized phrase? *Worth* is vague.)

Another cause of imprecise writing is misplaced and dangling modifers. With a misplaced modifier, the modifying word or phrase is not placed next to the sentence element it modifies, which leads to a confusing, and often humorous, result.

> Periodic inventory systems are often used by businesses that sell a large volume of inexpensive items *like grocery stores and drugstores.*
> (The italicized phrase appears to modify *items,* but it really modifies *businesses.*)
> Periodic inventory systems are often used by businesses, such as grocery stores and drugstores, which sell a large volume of inexpensive items.

Consider another sentence with a misplaced modifier:

> This technique identifies tax returns for audits with a high probability of error.

Revised:

> This technique identifies for audit tax returns with a high probability of error.

Dangling modifiers, which usually come at the beginning of a sentence, don't actually modify any word in the sentence. Usually the word modified is implied, rather than stated directly. Look at this sentence:

> After buying the bonds, the market price will fluctuate.

The writer probably meant something like:

> After we buy the bonds, the market price will fluctuate.

Faulty pronoun reference can also cause writing to be ambiguous and confusing:

> Capitalization of interest is adding interest to the cost of an asset under construction which increases its book value.

The meaning of this sentence is unclear. What increases book value? The pronoun *which* is confusing; its reference is vague.

Faulty pronoun reference can be labelled vague, ambiguous, or broad. These terms all mean that the writer doesn't make clear what the pronoun refers to. The pronoun *this* is particularly troublesome.

FAULTY REFERENCE: Generally Accepted Accounting Principles do not always indicate the true financial position of a company. This is a problem for the FASB.

REVISED: Generally Accepted Accounting Principles do not always indicate the true financial position of a company. This weakness in
the principles is a problem for the FASB.

A good rule is never to use *this* by itself. Add a noun or phrase to define what
this is.

Another pronoun that can cause problems with reference is *it:*

FAULTY REFERENCE: The inventory valuation can follow the physical flow of goods,
but it is not necessary.

REVISED: The inventory valuation can follow the physical flow of goods,
but this correspondence is not necessary.

Faulty diction, misplaced and dangling modifers, and faulty pronoun reference are grammatical problems. However, writing can be grammatically correct and
still be imprecise. Consider again this sentence:

The major drawback of the current value method is verifiability.

Revised:

The major drawback of the current value method is *the lack of* verifiability.

The revision makes quite a difference in meaning!

Often, the ability to write precisely is a function of precise reading—and
thinking. An accounting professor assigned his Accounting 801 students two papers
for the quarter. He then wrote the following statement on the board:

Accounting 801 students who complete the course will write a total of two papers this
quarter. True or false?

The precise thinkers in the class realized that the statement might not be true. The
students could write papers for other classes as well. Thus, some students could
write *more than* a total of two papers for the quarter.

Learn to analyze carefully what you read. Then you will be able to perfect
your own writing so that your meanings are clear and precise.

• • • • • •

This chapter has added six more techniques for effective writing:

1. **Analyze the purpose of the writing and the needs of the readers.**
2. **Use an outline to organize the ideas you want to present.**
3. **Write the rough draft, and revise it to make the writing polished and correct.**
4. **Unify the writing—all sentences should relate to the main idea, either directly or indirectly.**
5. **Use transitional expressions, repetition of key words and phrases, and pronouns to achieve coherent writing.**

6. Organize paragraphs by either a simple-deductive or a complex-deductive arrangement of supporting sentences.
7. Develop paragraphs by illustration, definition, detail, and appeals to authority.
8. Be concrete: use facts, details, and examples.
9. Use active voice whenever possible.
10. Keep it simple—simple vocabulary and short sentences.
11. Be concise—make every word count.
12. Vary vocabulary, sentence lengths, and sentence structures. Read the writing aloud to hear how it sounds.
13. Be precise—avoid ambiguous and confused meanings.

NOTES

1. H. Zane Robbins, "How to Develop Basic Writing Skills," *The Chronicle*, 40, no. 1 (1981), 11.
2. Richard A. Lanham, *Revising Prose* (New York: Charles Scribners Sons, 1979), p. 1.
3. George deMare, *How to Write and Speak Effectively* (New York: Price Waterhouse, 1958), p. 9.
4. Ibid., p. 11.
5. Adapted with permission of the publisher from *The Elements of Style*, Third Edition, by William Strunk, Jr. and E. B. White. Copyright © 1979 by Macmillan Publishing Co., Inc.
6. Adapted from Robert Gunning, *The Technique of Clear Writing* (New York: McGraw-Hill Book Company, Inc., rev. ed. 1968). Used by permission. "Fog Index" is a service mark of Gunning-Mueller Clear Writing Institute, Inc., Santa Barbara, California.
7. William E. Blundell, "Confused Overstuffed Corporate Writing Often Costs Firms Much Time—and Money," *The Wall Street Journal*, August 28, 1980, p. 21. Reprinted by permission of *The Wall Street Journal*, © Dow Jones and Company, Inc., 1980. All Rights Reserved.
8. The revised paragraph (see p. 63 of the Answers) is from Doug Hertha, "Audit Report of Charter Air" (unpublished student paper, University of Georgia, 1982).
9. The revised paragraph (see p. 63 of the Answers) is from Charles T. Horngren, *Introduction to Financial Accounting* (Englewood Cliffs, N.J.: Prentice-Hall, Inc., © 1981), p. 256. Reprinted by permission.
10. The revised paragraph (see p. 63 of the Answers) is from Howard F. Stettler, *Auditing Principles: A Systems-Based Approach* 5th ed. (Englewood Cliffs, N.J.: Prentice-Hall, Inc., © 1982), p. 47. Reprinted by permission.
11. Charles T. Horngren, *Introduction to Management Accounting*, 5th ed. (Englewood Cliffs, N.J.: Prentice-Hall, Inc., © 1981), p. 41. Reprinted by permission.
12. *Exxon Corporation 1980 Annual Report* (New York: Exxon Corporation, 1980), p. 10.
13. Wallace E. Olson, "Self-Regulation—What's Ahead?", *Journal of Accountancy*, 149, no. 3 (March 1980), 49.
14. *FASB Interpretation No. 7* (Stamford, Conn.: Financial Accounting Standards Board, 1975), para. 5. Copyright by Financial Accounting Standards Board, High Ridge Park,

Stamford, Connecticut, 06905, U.S.A. Reprinted with permission. Copies of the complete document are available from the FASB.

EXERCISES

Exercise 5-1

The following sentences are abstract or vague. Revise them, using facts, details, or examples to make them more concrete. You may need to replace one vague sentence with several concrete sentences, or even a short paragraph. Alternatively, you could introduce a short paragraph with an abstraction and then develop the idea with more concrete, specific sentences. Feel free to invent details that will make the ideas more specific.

Examples:

VAGUE: Accountants should write well.
REVISED: Accountants need to write clear, concise letters to their clients and other business associates. (This sentence replaces the vague *well* by indicating two characteristics of effective writing: clarity and conciseness. The revision also gives an example of one type of accountants' writing—letters to clients and associates.)
VAGUE: The financial statements are interesting.
REVISED: Smith Corporation's earnings statement for 19XX shows a net loss of $5,437,000.

OR

Smith Corporation's financial statements for 19XX contain information which stockholders may find alarming. For example, the earnings statement shows a net loss of $5,437,000.

1. Internal control is important.
2. Sometimes firms keep two sets of records.
3. We must record this asset at its true value. (Hint: what is "true value"?)
4. The audit didn't satisfy me.
5. The firm sold the asset for its cost. (Hint: what cost?)
6. Accounting for leases is tricky.
7. The nature of this asset requires us to capitalize it.
8. The accountant in charge of accounts receivable isn't doing his job.
9. These stocks look like a good buy.
10. Accountants must use good judgment.

Exercise 5-2

Identify the passive-voice constructions in the following sentences and revise them to active voice. Be careful not to substitute weak active verbs for passive voice. For some sentences you may need to invent a subject for the active verb.

Example:

PASSIVE: That alternative could have been followed.
ACTIVE: We (or the firm, our client, McDonough Corporation, etc.) could have followed
that alternative.

1. I have explained the three proposed alternatives for recording the cost of the equipment that has been purchased.
2. The option kept the land available until a decision was reached.
3. The accounts receivable aging is distorted by the journal entries.
4. Inventory should be controlled by the general ledger.
5. These disclosures are required for external reporting.
6. This procedure can easily be implemented.
7. It is recommended that finished parts inventories be physically controlled.
8. Most journal entries are reviewed by accounting management.
9. The opinion to be issued on the 19XX financial statements must be qualified.
10. Although our computer was purchased last year, it is already obsolete.
11. Each month our company's net income is reduced by accrued expenses.
12. At the seminar guidelines will be provided for lease accounting.
13. In many college accounting courses effective writing skills are emphasized.
14. Effective writing is needed in almost every aspect of business.
15. The prior years' working papers were reviewed.
16. No audit work was performed on internal control by our firm.
17. Questions about these plans should be directed to me immediately.
18. The second general standard of auditing requires that independence, both in fact and appearance, be maintained by the auditor.
19. These deferred expenses should have been recognized before this year.
20. The purpose of this memo is to discuss what kind of opinion should be issued by our firm for the audit of Brown Industries.
21. It is believed that this change in estimates has a material effect and therefore should be disclosed.
22. Our opinion on the financial statements may have to be modified.
23. In SAS No. 1 it is stated that items such as these must be disclosed in a footnote.
24. Our earnings statement was distorted by these incorrect figures.
25. When we purchased the building, it should have been recorded as an asset.

Exercise 5-3

Review the lists of simplified word choices on pp. 40–42 of this chapter. Then, without looking at the lists again, write a shorter and/or simpler version of the following words and phrases.

Example:

	Simplify to:
in all cases	always

1. i.e.
2. enclosed please find
3. facilitate
4. initiate
5. prior to
6. so as to
7. the major part of
8. make a purchase
9. make an analysis of
10. for the purpose of
11. in the amount of
12. optimum
13. maintain cost control
14. the writer
15. this is to acknowledge
16. under separate cover
17. with reference to
18. utilize
19. transpire
20. investigate
21. in the nature of
22. please be advised that
23. terminate
24 pursuant to your inquiry
25. failed to
26. at this point in time
27. in advance of
28. due to the fact that
29. exercise care
30. pertaining to
31. it should be noted that

Exercise 5-4

Revise the following sentences so that they are written as simply and concisely as possible. Be alert for hidden verbs.

A.

1. We should not make reference to prior years' financial statements in our report.
2. The history of Elliot Industry's performance, which is marginal at best, may be an indication of solvency problems that will occur in the future.
3. A number of problems have come to light that may make it necessary for us to issue an opinion that is other than unqualified.
4. I have attempted to explain the three proposed alternatives for recording the cost of the land that has been purchased.

5. It is my recommendation that New York Corporation choose to value the asset at $95,000.

6. As you are no doubt aware, in the economic environment of today, having these services available from a firm with experience is indispensable and quite valuable.

7. I am in need of improved writing skills.

8. In conclusion, I would like to state that I feel this seminar is an excellent opportunity.

9. There are several benefits that can come from attending the seminar.

10. I hope this memo will exhibit the reasons why the conference will be beneficial.

11. The benefits of this educational program will avail themselves to the corporation via language and letters which are fresh, accurate, and clear.

12. Per the discussion held with you during our recent visit, there are several control objectives within the above-mentioned cycles that need to have techniques established or refined to assure that these objectives are met.

13. These techniques will provide for an increased understanding of the problem.

14. Enclosed please find the information you will need to make an analysis of our inventory control.

15. We hope to begin production of our new product line before the end of the year.

16. Utilization of linear models alone may lead to unnecessary limitations as to the inferences that one may be able to draw from the data.

17. When executing the purchase of land, there are a number of costs incurred.

18. This method provides proper matching of expenses to revenues.

B.

1. Capitalizing the cost of options on land that is not purchased causes a misstatement of the true cost of land.

2. This method will result in a distribution of the costs between the balance sheet and the income statement.

3. This is to acknowledge receipt of your letter of June 1.

4. This is to inform you that we are sending a check in the amount $798.14.

5. We hope the entire staff will assist us in our efforts to reduce costs.

6. These classifications are required for external reporting purposes.

7. The accrual concept is the method that recognizes changes in the resources and obligations of an entity.

8. This memo will hopefully reveal that using this method serves the purpose of showing all expenses in the period when they occur.

9. Wordiness is the problem that makes my writing ineffective.

10. One can propose an argument that we should recognize the entire $10,000 in option costs as costs that relate to the $60,000 contract purchase price.

11. This memo will present supportive arguments for recording the asset at $100,000.

12. We are able to make the determination of the historical cost of an asset due to the fact that we have records of its purchase.

13. During the time that we were reviewing the statements for the purpose of our audit report, other members of our staff noticed a number of inconsistencies in the recording of transactions.

14. We will endeavor to complete our report prior to December 31.

15. The estimates range all the way from $100 to $350.
16. We don't have sufficient cash to make that investment at this point in time.
17. It is vital that I have your answer at your earliest convenience.
18. We don't expect problems in carrying out these changes.

Exercise 5-5

Identify the prepositional phrases in the following sentences. Where too many phrases are linked together, revise the sentence.

Example:

> The problem of Breland Company is solved through the selection of one of the accounting methods presented.
> Prepositional phrases identified:
>
> The problem (of) Breland Company, is solved (through) the selection (of) one (of) the accounting methods presented.

Revised:

> One of the accounting methods should solve Breland Company's problem.

1. Now that the choice of sites has been made and the expiration of options is occuring, this transaction must be recorded in the books of our firm correctly.
2. We have designed an audit program for use in future audits of the accounts receivable of ABC Company.
3. An accrual of expenses reports a more accurate picture of the operations of the current business period of the company.
4. The important issue to address in this company's situation is that of the expression of an opinion of the going concern.
5. The main problem of the staff is the determination of the cost at which to record the purchase.
6. The effect on our audit report of the sale of the bonds is twofold.
7. The return on an investment in bonds is based on the number of years to maturity and the current rate of interest in the market.
8. The calculation of the present values of the principal of the bonds and their cash flows will reveal our risk.
9. The amortization of the discount of the bond will allow us to realize the cash flows of the bond at an even rate throughout the life of the bond.
10. The determination of the net income of the company will pose no problems for the accountants in our department.

Exercise 5-6

Read the following paragraphs aloud; note their monotonous rhythms. Then revise the paragraphs so that they show greater variety in sentence structures and lengths. Note also when words or phrases are repeated too often.

1. Charter Air runs scheduled flights between several local communities. Charter Air also provides charter service for several local businesses. Charter's financial statements reveal marginal profits for the past several years. Last year Charter was forced to raise prices to compensate for increased fuel prices. These price increases and several economic downturns caused passenger volume to decline drastically. Thus 1979 was a disastrous year for Charter Air. The preliminary information showed that 1979 losses were in excess of $2,000,000. This will force Charter Air into a deficit position. The 1978 balance sheet showed a net worth of $2,000,000 with total assets of $10,000,000.[8]

2. Every business sells products that may be returned. The customers may be unhappy with the product for many reasons. The customer may not like the size, style, or color. The customer may also simply change his or her mind. The supplier (vendor) calls these sales returns. The customer calls them purchase returns. Such returns are minor for manufacturers and wholesalers. They are major for retail department stores. Marshall Field may have returns of 12 percent of gross sales.[9]

3. As a professional person, the CPA should serve his clients with competence and with professional concern for their best interests. At the same time, he must not permit his regard for a client's interest to override his independence, integrity, and objectivity. To discharge this dual responsibility, the accountant needs a high degree of ethical perception and conduct.[10]

Exercise 5-7

Revise the following paragraphs, using the techniques covered in this chapter as necessary.

1. If excess cash on hand is kept by a business, a loss for the business will result. Excess cash on hand brings in no benefits, while interest payments could be earned by the business. Investing cash on hand in government bonds would be a good thing for the company to do because it would be beneficial.

2. The purpose of this memo is an attempt to explain the three alternatives that have been proposed for recording the cost of the land that has been purchased by our company. The reasons for the recommendation I decided upon are discussed below along with the strong and weak points of the other proposed alternatives that I do not recommend. If one of these alternatives had been more consistent with GAAP, that alternative could have been followed.

3. In order to find a suitable site for our new plant, we purchased three options on three pieces of land. The costs of all three options are thought to be necessary to find a site that will be suitable for our new plant. Since it is not impossible that all the three option costs will contribute to the economic benefit and to the general well-being of our company in the future, the amount that should be capitalized by our company includes the costs of all three of the options. Even though the company will choose only one site for purchase and eventually build the plant on it, the amount we should capitalize includes the costs of all three options. The reasoning is that the company uses all the options to decide on the site for the new plant.

4. Per the discussion that was held with you by our audit staff during their recent communication with you at your Denver office, there are several objectives for control within several accounting cycles that need to have control techniques and procedures established or refined to ensure that these objectives are met by your company. It is vital that all the objectives of control within each of these cycles have control objectives established or improved to provide assurance that the objective is achieved by the

company in order to provide data that is accurate and timely, to preserve the integrity of the financial records of the company, and to maintain an adequate system of internal control, especially over the company's accounts receivable. In addition to the specific control techniques discussed in the following report, written procedures should be established so that data will be recorded in the way that management of the company intends.

Exercise 5-8

Compute the Fog Index on the following passages.

Example:

Variable costs (and *expenses*) and fixed costs (and *expenses*) have *contrasting behavior* patterns. Their *relationship* to sales, volume, and net profit is *probably* best seen on a cost-volume-profit graph. However, the graph should be used with great care. The *portrayal* of all profit-*influencing* factors on such a graph entails many *assumptions* that may hold over only a *relatively* narrow range of volume. As a tool, the graph may be compared to a meat-ax rather than to a surgeon's scalpel. Cost-volume-profit *analysis,* as depicted on a graph, is a framework for *analysis,* a *vehicle* for *appraising* overall *performance,* and a planning device.[11]

a. Average number of words per sentence:
    107 (total words) ÷ 6 (sentences) = 17.8 = 18
b. Percentage of words longer than two syllables (italicized):
    15 (big words) ÷ 107 (total words) − 14%
c. 14 (percentage of big words) + 18 (average sentence length) = 32
d. 0.4 × 32 = 12.8

Fog Index = 12

1. Refining and marketing earnings rose 18 percent. Improved margins offset the effect of lower sales volumes in virtually all markets. The year-to-year improvement in earnings was concentrated in the first half, reflecting the relatively depressed margins which had prevailed in the first half of 1979.

    Demand for petroleum products declined in most industrialized countries, variously reflecting the more efficient use of energy, substitution of other forms of energy and sluggish economies. During the first three quarters of 1980, Exxon's product inventories grew to historically high levels. They were partially drawn down following the outbreak of war between Iraq and Iran.[12] (*Note:* Count as words of one syllable *18, 1979, 1980.*)

2. It seems clear that we need to rethink and restructure our approach to self-regulation to make it more effective and to avoid duplication. In general, we ought to leave SEC client cases to the SEC section and refer as many private company cases to state boards of accountancy as they are willing and able to handle. We should downplay disciplinary action by the PCPS. We should go on the offensive to seek out cases of substandard work. The AICPA ethics division should be restructured to deal with the changed circumstances that now confront us, and we should seek the necessary council actions or bylaw changes to implement our revised approach to discipline.[13] (*Note:* Count as

words of one syllable *SEC, PCPS, AICPA*. The last sentence counts as two sentences because it contains two independent clauses.)

3. Except in the circumstances described in the preceding paragraph, the effect of a development stage subsidiary's change in accounting principle to conform its accounting to the requirements of *Statement No. 7* generally would be reflected in an established operating enterprise's consolidated financial statements that include that subsidiary. When a development stage subsidiary adopts a new accounting principle to conform its accounting to the requirements of *Statement No. 7*, and the effect of that subsidiary's accounting change is also reflected in an established operating enterprise's consolidated financial statements that include that subsidiary, the provisions of paragraph 14 of *Statement No. 7* apply.[14] (*Note:* Count as words of one syllable *No. 7* and *14.*)

Exercise 5-9

Compute the fog index on three samples of your own writing. Do you need to simplify your writing style?

Exercise 5-10

The meaning of the following sentences is not clear. Revise the sentences so that they are unambiguous and precise.

1. After reading the following discussion, a recommendation will present the best method for our company.
2. Each alternative has its rational for use.
3. The FASB has not officially written a pronouncement on the handling of acquisition costs.
4. Proponents claimed that the proposed legislation would provide changes from the old method of depreciation that would increase deductions and simplify computations.
5. The report was concerned with the Accelerated Cost Recovery System as introduced in the Economic Recovery Tax Act of 1981. Its purpose was. . . .
6. All companies incur expenses that do not provide future benefits to keep their business going to produce revenue.
7. Capitalization states that once a cost expires, we should capitalize expense.
8. Calculating the present value of the bonds' principal and future cash flows will determine our risk.
9. The riskiness of these bonds does not depend on their selling price.
10. Under LIFO the lower costs are assigned to inventory which causes the cost of inventory to increase.
11. This bond is not considered risky because it sells at only 70% of its maturity value.
12. The return of an investment in bonds is based on the number of years to maturity and the current market rate of interest.
13. Bonds are a unique opportunity because investors can purchase and exchange them on an exchange market.
14. The company's deficit position is due to increasing fuel prices and the company's response in increasing prices.

15. When purchasing bonds at a discount, the investment cost is less than the face value of the investment.
16. When reviewing the prior auditor's workpapers, no recognition of a possible obsolescence problem was found.
17. The value of an option is to buy land at a stated price.
18. Historical cost accounting has several problems which do not consider inflation and changing prices.

ANSWERS TO EXERCISES

Answers, Exercise 5-1

Answers will vary.

Answers, Exercise 5-2

Answers will vary, but here are some possibilities:

1. I have explained the three proposed alternatives for recording the cost of the equipment that our client has purchased.
2. The option kept the land available until we reached a decision.
3. The journal entries distort the accounts receivable aging.
4. The bookkeepers should use the general ledger to control inventories.
5. The SEC requires these disclosures for external reporting.
6. Management can easily implement this procedure.
7. The auditors recommend that we physically control finished parts inventories.
8. Accounting management reviews most journal entries.
9. We must qualify our opinion on the 19XX financial statements.
10. Although we purchased our computer last year, it is already obsolete.
11. Each month accrued expenses reduce our company's net income.
12. The seminar will provide guidelines for lease accounting.
13. Many college accounting courses emphasize effective writing skills.
14. Effective writing is important in almost every aspect of business.
15. We reviewed the prior years' working papers.
16. Our firm performed no audit work on internal control.
17. Please direct your questions about these plans to me immediately.
18. The second general standard of field work requires that the auditor maintain independence in both fact and appearance.
19. Allied Corporation should have recognized these expenses before this year.
20. The purpose of this memo is to discuss what kind of opinion our firm should issue for the audit of Brown Industries.
21. I believe that this change in estimates has a material effect; thus, our statements should disclose this information.
22. We may have to modify our opinion on the financial statements.

23. SAS No. 1 states that the financial statements must disclose items such as these.
24. These incorrect figures distorted our earnings statement.
25. When we purchased the building, we should have recorded it as an asset.

Answers, Exercise 5-3

1. that is
2. enclosed is
3. ease, simplify
4. begin
5. before
6. to
7. most of
8. buy
9. analyze
10. for
11. of, for
12. best
13. control cost
14. I, me
15. thank you for
16. by June 1, separately, tomorrow, by parcel post
17. about
18. use
19. happen
20. study
21. like
22. omit
23. end, stop
24. as you requested
25. didn't
26. now
27. before
28. because, since
29. be careful
30. about, for
31. omit

Answers, Exercise 5-4

A.
1. We should not refer to prior years' financial statements in our report.
2. Elliot Industry's history of marginal performance may indicate future solvency problems.

3. We have found several problems that may require us to issue a qualified opinion.
4. I have explained the three proposals for recording the cost of the purchased land.
5. I recommend that New York Corporation value the asset at $95,000.
6. In today's economic environment, having these services available from an experienced firm is invaluable.
7. I need improved writing skills.
8. In conclusion, this seminar is an excellent opportunity.
9. The seminar will benefit participants in several ways.
10. This memo will show why the conference will be beneficial.
11. The corporation will benefit if I attend the seminar because I will learn to make my memos and letters fresh, accurate, and clear.
12. During our recent visit we discussed the need for improved techniques to meet the control objectives within these cycles.
13. These techniques will help us understand the problem.
14. Enclosed is the information you will need to analyze our inventory control.
15. We hope to begin producing our new product line before the end of this year.
16. Use of linear models alone may limit unnecessarily the inferences we can draw from the data.
17. When a company buys land, it incurs a number of costs.
18. This method properly matches expenses with revenues.

B.

1. Capitalizing the cost of options on land not purchased misstates the land's cost.
2. This method will distribute the costs between the balance sheet and the income statement.
3. Thank you for your letter of June 1.
4. We're sending a check for $798.14.
5. We hope the entire staff will help us lower costs.
6. These classifications are required for external reporting.
7. The accrual concept recognizes changes in an entity's resources and obligations.
8. This memo will reveal that this method shows all expenses in the period when they occur.
9. Wordiness may make writing ineffective.
10. One can argue that we should recognize the entire $10,000 in option costs as related to the $60,000 contract purchase price.
11. I recommend recording the asset at $100,000.
12. We can easily determine an asset's historical cost because we have records of its purchase.
13. While we were reviewing the statements for our audit report, other staff members noticed several inconsistencies in the recording of transactions.
14. We will try to complete our report before December 31.
15. The estimates range from $100 to $350.
16. We don't have enough cash to make that investment now.
17. It is important that I have your answer promptly.
18. We don't anticipate problems in implementing these changes.

Answers, Exercise 5-5

1. Now that the choice of sites has been made and the expiration of options is occurring, this transaction must be recorded in the books of our firm correctly.
   Now that we have chosen the site and the options have expired, we must record the transaction correctly in our books.

2. We have designed an audit program for use in future audits of the accounts receivable of ABC Company.
   We have designed a program for future audits of ABC Company's accounts receivable.

3. An accrual of expenses reports a more accurate picture of the operations of the current business period of the company.
   Accrued expenses report a more accurate picture of the company's current operations.

4. The important issue to address in this company's situation is that of the expression of an opinion of the going concern.
   Before we can issue our opinion, we must decide if this company is indeed a going concern.
   Note: to address is an infinitive (a verb), not a prepositional phrase. However, too many infinitive phrases can also make a sentence awkward.

5. The main problem of the staff is the determination of the cost at which to record the purchase.
   The staff's main problem is determining the cost at which to record the purchase.

6. The effect on our audit report of the sale of the bonds is twofold.
   The bonds' sale has two effects on our audit report.

7. The return on an investment on bonds is based on the number of years to maturity and the current rate of interest in the market.
   The bond's return on investment is based on the number of years to maturity and the market rate of interest.

8. The calculation of the present value of the principal of the bonds and their future cash flows will reveal our risk.
   Calculating the present value of the bonds' principal and future cash flows will reveal our risk.

9. The amortization of the discount of the bond will allow us to realize the cash flows of the bond at an even rate throughout the life of the bond.
   Amortizing the bond discount will allow us to realize the bond's cash flows evenly throughout the bond's life.

10. The determination of the net income of the company will pose no problems for the accountants in our department.
    Determining the company's net income will pose no problems for our department's accountants.

Answers, Exercise 5-6

1. Charter Air runs scheduled flights between several of the local communities in the area and provides charter service for several local businesses. According to its previous financial statements, Charter Air has been marginally profitable in the past several years. During the past year, Charter Air was forced to raise its prices to compensate for increased fuel costs. Because of these price increases and the effects of the general economic downturns, passenger volume declined drastically, making 19X9 a disastrous year for the company. The preliminary information showed that 19X9 losses

were in excess of $2,000,000. This will force Charter Air into a deficit position, as the 19X8 balance showed a net worth of $2,000,000 with total assets of $10,000.000.

2. Every business sells products that may be returned. The customer may be unhappy with the product for many reasons, including color, size, style, quality, and simply changing of the mind. The supplier (vendor) calls these sales returns; the customer calls them purchase returns. Such returns are minor for manufacturers and wholesalers but are major for retail department stores. For instance, returns of 12 percent of gross sales are not abnormal for stores like Marshall Field.

3. As a professional person, the CPA should serve his clients with competence and with professional concern for their best interests. He must not permit his regard for a client's interest, however, to override his obligation to the public to maintain his independence, integrity, and objectivity. The discharge of this dual responsibility to both clients and the public requires a high degree of ethical perception and conduct.

Answers, Exercise 5-7

The answers to this exercise will vary. The following lists identify the major weaknesses in each paragraph.

1. Passive voice, repetition of phrases, vague sentence.
2. Wordy, hedging, passive voice.
3. Repetitive, passive voice, wordy, too many prepositional phrases, sentences too long.
4. Wordy, passive voice, repetitive, sentences too long, verbs need simplifying.

Answers, Exercise 5-8

1. 14
2. 13
3. 1/+

Answers, Exercise 5-10

1. The following discussion will conclude with a recommended method.
2. Each alternative has its rationale for use.
3. The FASB has not written an official pronouncement on the handling of acquisition costs.
4. Proponents claimed that the proposed legislation would provide changes from the old method of depreciation; these changes would increase deductions and simplify computations.
5. The report was concerned with the Accelerated Cost Recovery System as introduced in the Economic Recovery Tax Act of 1981. The purpose of the report was. . . .
6. All companies incur expenses that do not provide future benefits, yet these expenses keep the business going by producing revenue.
7. The rule for capitalization states that once a cost expires, we should capitalize the expense.
8. Calculating the present value of the bonds' principal and future cash flows will reveal our risk.
9. The selling price of these bonds does not indicate their riskiness.

10. Because LIFO assigns lower costs to inventory, the cost of goods sold increases.
11. The selling price of this bond, which is 70% of its maturity value, does not necessarily indicate that the bond is risky.
12. The return on an investment in bonds is based on the number of years to maturity and the current market rate of interest at the time the bond was purchased.
13. Bonds are a good opportunity because investors can purchase and exchange them on an exchange market. (*Unique* means "one of a kind.")
14. The company is in a deficit position for two reasons: fuel prices increased, and the company increased its own prices in response to these rising fuel prices.
15. When bonds sell at a discount, the investment cost is less than the face value of the investment.
16. When reviewing the prior auditor's workpapers, we found no recognition of a possible obsolescence problem.
17. The value of an option is the ability it gives the holder to buy land at a stated price.
18. Historical cost accounting causes several problems because it does not take into account inflation and changing prices.

Chapter 6

GRAMMAR, PUNCTUATION, AND SPELLING

Grammar, punctuation, and spelling are the technical details of good writing. Sometimes the rules seem trivial and illogical, but for the most part they will help you achieve clarity and precision.

Accountants should have no trouble with precise detail. Think about how important the tiny decimal point is in a numerical figure! Punctuation marks can be just as important. Lawyers tell stories about misplaced commas in contracts costing clients thousands of dollars. Even though good punctuation, spelling, and grammar are seldom so dramatically important, they do contribute to polished, professional writing. Responsible accountants want all the details properly stated on a financial statement; it is also important that they use correct grammar and mechanics in their writing.

This chapter presents some of the most commonly made errors in grammar, punctuation, and spelling. Of course, only a few principles can be covered in this short space, so you should consult a basic English handbook for a complete list of rules and explanations. The discussion here focuses on rules that give accountants the most trouble.

COMMA SPLICES

Independent clauses can be combined correctly in three ways. When they are joined by a comma alone, the result is a comma splice, which is a major sentence error.

An independent clause is a group of words with a subject and a verb; it can stand alone as a sentence. Here are two independent clauses punctuated as separate sentences:

> Increases in assets are recorded as debits on the left side of a T-account. Decreases are recorded as credits on the right side.

Sometimes writers want to combine two independent clauses into one sentence. This can be correctly done in several ways.

1. Put a semi-colon (;) between the clauses.
   Increases in assets are recorded as debits on the left side of a T-account; decreases are recorded as credits on the right side.
2. Combine the clauses with a comma and a coordinating conjunction (*and, but, for, or, nor, yet, so*).
   Increases in assets are recorded as debits on the left side of a T-account, and decreases are recorded as credits on the right side.
3. Combine the clauses with a semi-colon, a conjunctive adverb, and a comma. (Conjunctive adverbs include *however, therefore, thus, consequently, that is, for example, nevertheless, also, furthermore, indeed, instead, still.*)
   Increases in assets are recorded as debits on the left side of a T-account; however, the decreases are recorded as credits on the right side.

Study the following comma splices. The independent clauses are joined by a comma alone.

INCORRECT: Accountants must not only understand accounting procedures, they must also be able to communicate effectively.

CORRECT: Accountants must not only understand accounting procedures; they must also be able to communicate effectively.
Accountants must understand accounting procedures and be able to communicate effectively.

INCORRECT: LIFO usually results in a lower net income, therefore, a company has lower income tax liabilities.

CORRECT: LIFO usually results in lower net income; therefore, a company has lower income tax liabilities.

SUBJECT-VERB AGREEMENT

A verb should agree with its subject in number. That is, singular subjects take singular verbs; plural subjects take plural verbs. Note that singular verbs in the present tense end in *s:*

> That (one) <u>man works</u> hard.
> Those (two) <u>men work</u> hard.

Some irregular verbs (*to be, to have,* etc.) look different, but you will probably recognize singular and plural forms.

> That <u>stock is</u> a good investment.
> These <u>stocks are</u> risky.
> The <u>ABC Corporation has</u> fifty accountants on its staff.
> Some <u>corporations have</u> net earnings of more than a million dollars.

There are a few difficulties with this rule. First, some singular subjects are often thought of as plural. *Each, every, either, neither, one, everybody,* and *anyone* take singular verbs.

> <u>Each</u> of the divisions <u>is</u> responsible for maintaining accounting records.

Second, sometimes phrases coming between the subject and the verb make agreement tricky.

> The <u>procedure</u> used today by most large companies in their foreign divisions <u>is explained</u> in this article.

Finally, two or more subjects joined by *and* take a plural verb. When subjects are joined by *or,* the verb agrees with the subject closest to it.

> Either <u>Company A</u> or <u>Company B is planning</u> to issue new stocks.
> Either the <u>president</u> or the <u>managers have called</u> this meeting.

PRONOUNS

Pronouns cause two main problems, agreement and reference. Agreement is easy: a pronoun should agree with its antecedent (the word it stands for). Thus singular antecedents take singular pronouns, and plural antecedents take plural pronouns.

> <u>Mr. Jones</u> took <u>his</u> check to the bank.

This rule usually gives trouble only with particular words. Note that *company, corporation, firm, management,* and *board* are singular; therefore, they take singular pronouns.

> The <u>company</u> increased <u>its</u> profits by fifty percent. (Not *company—their.*)
> The Accounting Principles <u>Board</u> discussed accounting for intangible assets in <u>its</u> Opinion No. 17. (Not *Board—their.*)

The second problem with pronouns is vague, ambiguous, or broad reference. This problem was discussed in Chapter 5.

APOSTROPHES AND PLURALS

The rules for apostrophes and plurals are quite simple, but many people get them confused.

Most plurals are formed by adding either *s* or *es* to the end of the word. If you're unsure of a plural spelling, consult a dictionary.

With one exception, apostrophes are never used to form plurals. Apostrophes are used to show possession. For singular words the form is *'s*. For plural words the apostrophe comes after the *s*.

SINGULAR	**PLURAL**
firm's capital	officers' salaries
statement's figures	users' interests
business's profits	businesses' profits

A commonly made mistake is *stockholders' equity*. When *stockholder(s)* is plural (it usually is), the apostrophe comes after the *s*.

There is one exception to the plural-apostrophe rule. Abbreviations, numerals, and letters can form their plurals with *'s:*

1980's or 1980s
CPA's or CPAs

Often a phrase requiring an apostrophe can be rewritten using *of* or its equivalent.

the company's statements (the statements of the company)
the month's income (the income of the month)
a week's work (the work of a week)
the year's total (the total for the year)

And note these possessive plurals:

two companies' statements
five months' income
three weeks' work
ten years' total
prior years' statements

"Ten years' total" might also be written "ten-year total." But analyze the difference in meaning between "ten-year total" and "ten years' totals."

Finally, some writers confuse *it's* with *its*. *It's* is a contraction of *it is; its* is the possessive pronoun.

It's important to make careful journal entries.

The company issued its statements.

COMMAS

The many rules for comma usage are sometimes hard to understand. However, commas are important for at least two reasons. First, when they are correctly placed, they make written material easier to read. Second, when they are incorrectly placed, they sometimes distort meaning. Consider the following example.

Gains on treasury stock were credited to a revenue account which is not an accepted practice.

This sentence does not make clear *what* is not an accepted practice. The revenue account? Or the practice of accounting for gains on treasury stock as a revenue? The meaning is much clearer if we add a comma.

Gains on treasury stock were credited to a revenue account, which is not an accepted practice.

Comma Guidesheet

Use Commas:

1. before *and, but, or, nor, for, so,* and *yet*—when these words come between independent clauses.
   The FASB issued a Discussion Memorandum, and many accountants responded with their opinions.
2. following an introductory adverbial clause.
   When investors read a company's financial statements, they are especially interested in the net income figure.
3. following long introductory phrases and transitional expressions.
   In the Statement of Financial Accounting Standards No. 2 (SFAS No. 2), the FASB defined its position on research and development costs.
4. to separate items in a series (including coordinate adjectives).
   Accounting students must be intelligent, dedicated, and conscientious.
5. to set off nonrestrictive clauses and phrases (compare rule 4, below).
   The SEC, which is an agency of the federal government, is concerned with proper presentation of financial statements.
6. to set off contrasted elements.
   Treasury stock is a capital account, not an asset.
7. to set off parenthetical elements.
   Changes in accounting methods, however, must be disclosed in the financial statements.

Do Not Use Commas:

1. to separate the subject from the verb or the verb from its complement.
   Incorrect:
   The company that manufacturers trucks, has an impressive net income.
   Correct:
   The company that manufactures trucks has an impressive net income.
2. to separate compound verbs or objects.
   Incorrect:
   He wrote angry letters to the FASB, and the SEC.
   Correct:
   He wrote angry letters to the FASB and the SEC.
3. to set off words and short phrases that are not parenthical.
   Incorrect:
   Financial transactions are recorded, in journals, in chronological order.
   Correct:
   Financial transactions are recorded in journals in chronological order.
4. to set off restrictive clauses, phrases, or appositives (compare rule 5, above).
   Incorrect:
   A problem, that concerns many accountants, is the use of historical cost in times of inflation.
   Correct:
   A problem that concerns many accountants is the use of historical cost in times of inflation.
5. before the first item or after the last item of a series (including coordinate adjectives).
   Incorrect:
   Some asset accounts are noncurrent, such as, land, buildings, and equipment.
   (The faulty comma is the one before *land.*)
   Correct:
   Some asset accounts are noncurrent, such as land, buildings, and equipment.

COLONS

The rules of colons (:) are few and easy to master, although sometimes writers use them incorrectly. Used correctly—and sparingly—colons can be effective because they draw the readers' attention to the material that follows.

Colons can be used in the following situations:

1. to introduce a series.
   Three new CPA firms have located in this area recently: Smith and Harrison, CPAs; Thomas R. Becker and Associates; and Johnson & Baker, CPAs.
2. to introduce a direct quotation, especially a long quotation that is set off from the main body of the text (see the following section).
   The senior partner issued the following instruction:
   All audit workpapers should include concise, well-organized memos summarizing any problem revealed by the audit.
3. to emphasize a summary or explanation.

My investigation of Ace Manufacturing's financial situation led me to an important conclusion: Unless Ace attracts new capital immediately, it may be forced into bankrupcy.

4. following the salutation in a business letter.
   Dear Mr. Evans:

When a colon introduces a series, an explanation, or a summary, the clause that precedes the colon should be a complete statement:

We have increased our sales to the following customers: Elliot Industries, Anderson, Inc., and Trueblood Manufacturing.

Not

Our best customers are: Elliot Industries, Anderson, Inc., and Trueblood Manufacturing.

DIRECT QUOTATIONS

The punctuation of direct quotations depends on their length. Short quotations (less than five typed lines) are run on in the main body of the text and enclosed with quotation marks. Longer quotations are set off from the text—indented and single spaced—with no quotation marks. Longer quotations should be formally introduced; a colon separates the introduction from the quoted material. Study the following examples:

In SFAS No. 14, the FASB defines an industry segment as a "component of an enterprise engaged in providing a product or service or a group of related products or services primarily to unaffiliated customers . . . for a profit."[1]

In SFAS No. 14, the FASB gives the following definition of an industry segment:

Industry segment. A component of an enterprise engaged in providing a product or service or a group of related products and services primarily to unaffiliated customers (i.e., customers outside the enterprise) for a profit. By defining an industry segment in terms of products and services that are sold primarily to unaffiliated customers, this Statement does not require the disaggregation of the vertically integrated operations of an enterprise.[2]

A direct quotation requires a footnote identifying its source (see Chapter 11). In addition, it is better to identify briefly the source of a quotation within the text itself, as the above examples illustrate. If a quotation comes from an individual, use his or her complete name the first time you quote from this source.

According to Richard Smith, an executive officer of the Fairways Corporation, "The industry faces an exciting challenge in meeting foreign competition."

Notice the placement of punctuation in relation to quotation marks:
    Inside quotation marks:

period   quotation.''
comma   quotation,''

    Outside quotation marks:

colon   quotation'':
semi-colon   quotation'';

    Inside or outside quotations marks:

question mark ?'' or ''?
— depending on whether the question mark is part of the original quotation:
Mr. Misel asked, ''Where is the file of our new client?''
Did Mr. Misel say, ''I have lost the file of our new client''?

One final remark. Sometimes writers depend too heavily on direct quotation. It is usually better to paraphrase—to express someone else's ideas in your own words—unless precise quotation would be an advantage. As a rule, no more than twenty percent of a paper should be direct quotation. To be most effective, quotations should be used sparingly, and then only for authoritative support or dramatic effect.

SPELLING

Finished, revised writing should be entirely free of misspelled words. Keep a dictionary on your desk, and use it if you have any doubt about a word's spelling.

Spelling: If in Doubt, Look It Up!

The following short list contains words commonly misspelled by accountants:

accrual, accrued
advise/advice
affect/effect
cost/costs, consist/consists, risk/risks
led, misled
occurred, occurring, occurrence
principal/principle
receivable, receive
separate, separately
. . . .

The italicized words in the following sentences are frequently confused.

Please *advise* us of your decision. (*Advise* is a verb).

We appreciate your *advice*. (*Advice* is a noun).

This change in accounting policy will not *affect* the financial statements. (*Affect* is a verb).

This change in accounting policy will have no *effect* on the financial statements. (*Effect* is usually a noun. Rarely, *effect* is a verb meaning "to cause to happen.")

The *cost* of the new machine is more than we expected. (*Cost* is singular).

The *costs* of these assets are not recorded correctly. (*Costs* is plural, but when you say the word aloud, you can't hear the final *s*.)

This ambiguous footnote may *mislead* investors. (*Mislead* is present or future tense.)

This ambiguous footnote *misled* investors. (*Misled* is past tense.)

How should we record the *principal* of this bond investment?

This procedure does not follow Generally Accepted Accounting *Principles*.

In summary, good grammar, punctuation, and spelling are essential for polished, professional writing. Don't just guess about the rules; resolve your uncertainties with a grammar handbook or dictionary. Remember the needs of your readers. Correct grammar and mechanics are necessary for smooth, clear reading.

A final word: It is important to proofread your finished product for typographical errors—whether you or someone else does the actual typing. Typing errors make work look sloppy, and the writer seem careless. Effective writing should look professional: correct, neat, and polished.

This chapter has given the final rule for effective writing.

1. **Analyze the purpose of the writing and the needs of the readers.**
2. **Use an outline to organize the ideas you want to present.**
3. **Write the rough draft, and revise it to make the writing polished and correct.**
4. **Unify the writing—all sentences should relate to the main idea, either directly or indirectly.**
5. **Use transitional expressions, repetition of key words and phrases, and pronouns to achieve coherent writing.**
6. **Organize paragraphs by either a simple-deductive or a complex-deductive arrangement of supporting sentences.**
7. **Develop paragraphs by illustration, definition, detail, and appeals to authority.**
8. **Be concrete: use facts, details, and examples.**
9. **Use active voice whenever possible.**
10. **Keep it simple—simple vocabulary and short sentences.**
11. **Be concise—make every word count.**
12. **Vary vocabulary, sentence lengths, and sentence structures. Read the writing aloud to hear how it sounds.**
13. **Be precise—avoid ambiguous and confused meanings.**
14. **Pooofread for grammar, punctuation, spelling, and typographical errors.**

NOTES

1. *Statement of Financial Accounting Standards No. 14: Financial Reporting for Segments of a Business Enterprise* (Stamford, Conn.: Financial Accounting Standards Board, 1976), para. 10a. Copyright by Financial Accounting Standards Board, High Ridge Park, Stamford, Connecticut, 06905, U.S.A. Reprinted with permission. Copies of the complete document are available from the FASB.
2. Ibid.

EXERCISES

Exercise 6-1

Join these independent classes together in three ways.

under variable costing a company's sales will influence income
under absorption costing both sales and production will affect income.

Exercise 6-2

Identify and correct any comma splices you find in the following sentences.

1. Tinto Paint may argue that these costs do not provide future benefits, thus, Tinto may choose to expense them.
2. Ethel Corporation must not only improve its internal control system, it must also review its procedures for accounts receivable.
3. Many types of users rely on financial statement information, for example, creditors use the information to evaluate a firm's credit worthiness.
4. Physical volume is one factor that affects cost behavior; other factors include efficiency, changes in technology, unit prices of inputs, etc.
5. The main reason for our concern, however, is the incorrect recording of accounts receivable.
6. Accountants do not depreciate land, therefore, we cannot allocate land costs on a systematic and rational basis.
7. Historical cost usually results from arms'-length transactions and therefore provides reliable measures of transactions.
8. The FASB recognizes that the present financial statements do not reflect changing prices and inflation, thus the FASB is working on acceptable ways to account for changing prices.
9. Although we discussed this policy at the May meeting, some staff members still do not understand it.
10. Since historical cost financial statements do not show the effects of inflation, some accountants advocate constant dollar accounting.

Exercise 6-3

Some of these sentences have errors in subject-verb agreement. Identify these errors and correct the sentences.

1. Changes in the general purchasing power of the dollar forces accountants to deal with an unstable monetary unit.

2. Neither the president nor the supervisors understand the new policy.
3. One problem we found in our reviews of the records were that revenues were not always recorded in the proper period.
4. A statement with supplementary disclosures provide additional information to investors.
5. The physical flow of goods generally follow the FIFO pattern.
6. Each of these statements is prepared according to GAAP.
7. Neither the president nor the controller understand the new policy.
8. The future benefits provided by the bond is partly due to its high interest rate.
9. Restating asset values to current costs results in realized and unrealized holding gains and losses.
10. Due to the changing value of the dollar, meaningful interpretation of historical cost statements and comparisons among firms has become nearly impossible.

Exercise 6-4

Correct any pronoun errors you find in the following sentences.

1. When an investor or creditor wishes to compare two companies, they cannot always rely on the historical cost statements for the comparison.
2. Ace Manufacturing should remember that they are allowed to expense the cost of certain property.
3. The FASB deals with research and development costs in their Statement No. 2.
4. Management is interested in improving the revenue figures for their report to the stockholders.
5. Each accountant is required to complete his report on time.
6. The Smallwood Corporation has greatly increased it's advertising expense.
7. A switch to LIFO usually results in a lower income tax liability and a lower inventory figure on the balance sheet; this would be important to our company.
8. The Board of Directors will hold its next meeting in July.
9. Every corporation coming under SEC regulations must follow certain procedures in preparing their financial statements.
10. Everyone registering for the convention will receive a package of information when they arrive.

Exercise 6-5

a. Complete the following chart.

Singular	Singular Possessive	Plural	Plural Possessive
statement			
company			
business			
cost			
risk			
CPA			
year			
industry			

    b. Use the words from the chart to fill in these sentences. The singular form of the correct word is given in the parentheses.

1. (CPA) _____ from all over the country will be at the convention.
2. (business) Investors examine a _____ statements to determine its financial condition.
3. (cost) Record all these _____ in the proper amounts.
4. (statement) Which of the _____ is in error?
5. (cost) What is the replacement _____ of this machine?
6. (risk) Investors in these bonds must accept certain _____.
7. (industry) Research and development are crucial in many _____.
8. (year) We should see a profit in two _____ time.
9. (company) The Board of Directors considered the _____ pension plan.
10. (statement) We are making changes in the two _____ totals.

Exercise 6-6

Punctuate the following sentences correctly.

1. When the Board of Directors met in December the company showed a net loss of $5,000,000.
2. To increase the revenues from its new product the company introduced an advertising campaign in New York Chicago and Los Angeles.
3. The biggest problem in our firm however is obsolete inventories.
4. We currently value our inventories according to LIFO not FIFO.
5. For example Elixir Products should consider FASB Statement No. 13 which deals with leases.
6. The auditors revealed several problems in Thompson Company's financial records such as its depreciation policy its handling of bad debts and its inventory accounting.
7. The presidents letter contained the following warning "If our revenues don't increase soon the plant may be forced to close"
8. "We're planning a new sales strategy" the manager wrote in reply.
9. We have decided not to invest in the Allied bonds at this time instead we are considering Blackstone's common stocks.
10. Although our revenues increased during June expenses rose at an alarming rate.

Exercise 6-7

Identify and correct any misspelled words in the following list. Look up any words you are unsure of; not all of these words were included in the chapter.

1. believe
2. receive
3. occured
4. seperate
5. accural
6. benefitted

7.   existance
8.   principle (the rule)
9.   cost (plural)
10. mislead (past tense)
11. advise (the noun)
12. affect (the verb)

Exercise 6-8

Correct all errors in the following paragraph.

Most company's base asset values on their historical cost, however, historical cost have become outdated with the rising prices in todays economy. This creates a problem for investors, investors should know the costs the corporation will have to incur if they are to continue operations. When investors are presented with this information they can better understand the affects of inflation and the need to retain some reported earnings in the business. To provide this important information to investors we at Elliot Industries should present supplementary data in our financial statements.

ANSWERS TO EXERCISES

Answers, Exercise 6-1

Under variable costing a company's sales will influence income; under absorption costing both sales and production will affect income.
Under variable costing a company's sales will influence income, but under absorption costing both sales and production will affect income.
Under variable costing a company's sales will influence income; however, under absorption costing both sales and production will affect income.

Answers, Exercise 6-2

1.   Comma splice. Correction:
     Tinto Paint may argue that these costs do not provide future benefits; thus, Tinto may choose to expense them.

                                OR

     Tinto Paint may argue that these costs do not provide future benefits. Thus, Tinto may choose to expense them.

NOTE: Some of the following comma splices can be corrected in more than one way. However, this key will give only one possible correction. If you recognize the comma splice, you probably understand how to correct it.

2. Comma splice. Correction:
   Ethel Corporation must not only improve its internal control system; it must also review its procedures for accounts receivable.

3. Comma splice. Correction:
   Many types of users rely on financial statement information; for example, creditors use the information to evaluate a firm's credit worthiness.

4. Correct.

5. Correct. (*However* doesn't come between two independent clauses in this sentence.)

6. Comma splice. Correction:
   Accountants do not depreciate land. Therefore, we cannot allocate land costs on a systematic and rational basis.

7. Correct. (*Therefore* doesn't come between two independent clauses.)

8. Comma splice. Correction:
   The FASB recognizes that the present financial statements do not reflect changing prices and inflation; thus, the FASB is working on acceptable ways to account for changing prices.

9. Correct. (The first clause—"although we discussed this policy at the May meeting,"—is not independent; it could not stand alone as a sentence.)

10. Correct. (The first clause is not independent.)

Answers, Exercise 6-3

1. Changes in the general purchasing power of the dollar *force* accountants to deal with an unstable monetary unit. (The verb should agree with the subject *changes.*)

2. Correct.

3. One problem we found in our reviews of the records *was* that revenues were not always recorded in the proper period. (The verb should agree with *problem.*)

4. A statement with supplementary disclosures *provides* additional information to investors. (The verb should agree with *statement.*)

5. The physical flow of goods generally *follows* the FIFO pattern. (The verb should agree with *flow.*)

6. Correct.

7. Neither the president nor the controller *understands* the new policy. (The verb should agree with *controller.*)

8. The future benefits provided by the bond *are* partly due to its high interest rate. (The verb should agree with *benefits.*)

9. Correct.

10. Due to the changing value of the dollar, meaningful interpretation of historical cost statements and comparisons among firms *have* become nearly impossible. (The verb should agree with *interpretation . . . and comparisons.*)

Answers, Exercise 6-4

1. When an investor or creditor wishes to compare two companies, *he* cannot always rely on the historical cost statements for the companies. (Alternatives: *he or she; investors or creditors/they*).

2. Ace Manufacturing should remember that *it* is allowed to expense the cost of certain property.
3. The FASB deals with research and development costs in *its* Statement No. 2.
4. Management is interested in improving the revenue figures for *its* report to the stockholders.
5. Correct.
6. The Smallwood Corporation has greatly increased *its* advertising expense.
7. A switch to LIFO usually results in a lower income tax liability and a lower inventory figure on the balance sheet; these advantages would be important to our company.
8. Correct.
9. Every corporation coming under SEC regulations must follow certain procedures in preparing *its* financial statements.
10. Everyone registering for the convention will receive a package of information when *he or she* arrives. (Alternative: *he*).

Answers, Exercise 6-5

a. Singular	Singular Possessive	Plural	Plural Possessive
statement	statement's	statements	statements'
company	company's	companies	companies'
business	business's	businesses	businesses'
cost	cost's	costs	costs'
risk	risk's	risks	risks'
CPA	CPA's	CPAs or CPA's	CPAs'
year	year's	years	years'
industry	industry's	industries	industries'

b.

1. CPA's or CPAs
2. business's
3. costs
4. statements
5. cost
6. risks
7. industries
8. years'
9. company's
10. statements'

Answers, Exercise 6-6

1. When the Board of Directors met in December, the company showed a net loss of $5,000,000.
2. To increase the revenues from its new product, the company introduced an advertising campaign in New York, Chicago, and Los Angeles.

3.   The biggest problem in our firm, however, is obsolete inventories.
4.   We currently value our inventories according to LIFO, not FIFO.
5.   For example, Elixir Products should consider FASB Statement No. 13, which deals with leases.
6.   The auditors revealed several problems in Thompson Company's financial records, such as its depreciation policy, its handling of bad debts, and its inventory accounting.
7.   The president's letter contained the following warning: "If our revenues don't increase soon, the plant may be forced to close."
8.   "We're planning a new sales strategy," the manager wrote in reply.
9.   We have decided not to invest in the Allied bonds at this time. Instead, we are considering Blackstone's common stocks. (Alternative: We have decided not to invest in the Allied bonds at this time; instead, we are considering Blackstone's common stocks.)
10. Although our revenues increased during June, expenses rose at an alarming rate.

Answers, Exercise 6-7

1.   correct
2.   correct
3.   occurred
4.   separate
5.   accrual
6.   benefited
7.   existence
8.   correct
9.   costs
10. misled
11. advice
12. correct

Answer, Exercise 6-8

Most companies base asset values on their historical costs; however, historical costs have become outdated with the rising prices in today's economy. This failure to reflect inflation creates a problem for investors. Investors should know the costs the corporation will have to incur if it is to continue operations. When investors are presented with this information, they can better understand the effects of inflation and the need to retain some reported earnings in the business. To provide this important information to investors, we at Elliot Industries should present supplementary data in our financial statements.

Chapter 7

ESSAYS: AN APPROACH TO ORGANIZATION AND DEVELOPMENT

A chapter entitled "Essays" might sound too academic for a writing handbook for accountants. The chapter is included here, however, for two reasons. First, the CPA exam contains essay questions, and many accounting students and recent graduates need guidance in answering these questions effectively. Second, many of the basic principles of organizing and developing an essay are applicable to memos, reports, and other types of writing used by accountants in actual practice.

This chapter begins with a brief section on short discussion questions, followed by a closer look at the organization and development of a longer essay.

SHORT DISCUSSION QUESTIONS

The key to answering a one- or two-paragraph discussion question is well-organized paragraphs with strong topic sentences (see Chapter 4). Sometimes the question itself will suggest the topic sentence. For example, consider the question:

Discuss who the users of financial statements are.

The answer to this question might begin with the following sentence.

The users of an organization's financial statements are mainly external to the organization.

The first paragraph of the answer would discuss external users—investors, creditors, government agencies, etc. A second, shorter paragraph might then discuss internal users of financial statements—management, employees, etc. The second topic sentence might be as follows.

People within an organization are also interested in its financial statements.

ESSAYS

Before you read this section, go back and review the section in Chapter 4 on paragraph development; pay particular attention to the complex-deductive pattern of organization.

Complex-deductive paragraphs have a main idea (topic sentence) supported by major and minor supports. Essays—discussions of four or more paragraphs—are organized the same way, except that the main idea (thesis statement) has as its major supports paragraphs rather than sentences. In addition, the thesis statement comes at the end of the first paragraph; it is preceded by attention-getting sentences. Here is the basic outline of a five-paragraph essay:

   I. Introduction—first paragraph
      A. Attention-getting sentences
      B. Thesis statement—main idea of the essay, usually expressed in one sentence
  II. Body of the essay—develops the thesis through analysis, explanation, examples, proofs, or steps
      A. Major support—second paragraph
         1.
         2.   Minor supports—sentences which develop the paragraph in a simple-
               or complex-deductive organization
         3. etc.
      B. Major support—third paragraph
         1.
         2.   minor supports
         3.
      C. Major support—fourth paragraph
         1.
         2.   minor supports
         3.
 III. Conclusion—fifth paragraph
      A. Repeats the essay's main idea—a variation of the thesis statement
      B. Forceful ending

Some of the parts of this outline need more discussion.

Attention-getting
Sentences

The purpose of the attention-getting sentences is to get the reader interested in the subject. Several techniques can be used:

- Give background information about the topic. Why is the topic of current interest?
- Pose a problem or raise a question (to be answered in the essay).
- Define key terms, perhaps the topic itself.
- Show the relevance of the topic to the reader.
- Begin with an interesting direct quotation.
- Relate a brief anecdote relevant to the topic.
- Relate the specific topic to a wider area of interest.

The following introduction to an essay on the monetary unit assumption uses two of these techniques. The paragraph begins with a brief background of the topic; it then suggests the relevance of this topic for present study and concludes with a thesis statement.

> One of the basic assumptions accountants made in the past was that money was an effective common denominator by which business enterprises could be measured and analyzed. Implicit in this assumption is the acceptance of the stable and unchanging nature of monetary units. Recently, however, the validity of this assumption has been questioned not only by academicians and theorists, but by practitioners as well. From these questions accountants have developed several methods to adjust and correct for the floating nature of the monetary unit.[1]

Notice how smoothly the attention-getting sentences flow into the thesis statement. Be careful that there is not an abrupt jump in these two parts of the introduction. You may need to use a transition such as the one in the above paragraph ("From these questions . . .").

Thesis Statement

The thesis statement summarizes the main idea of the essay, usually in one sentence. It may be a *simple* thesis statement, such as the one just studied.

> From these questions accountants have developed several methods to adjust and correct for the floating nature of the monetary unit.

Alternatively, the thesis statement may be *expanded*. That is, it may summarize the main supports of the discussion.

> Two methods developed to correct for an unstable monetary unit are the general purchasing power approach and current value accounting.

Sometimes, to avoid a long or awkward sentence, you may want to use two sentences for the thesis statement.

From these questions accountants have developed several methods to adjust and correct for the floating nature of the monetary unit. Two of these methods are the general purchasing power approach and current value accounting.

Conclusion

The conclusion must do at least one thing: repeat the discussion's main idea, usually in some variation of the thesis statement. In addition, effective conclusions often end with a forceful statement that will stay in the reader's mind, thus giving the discussion a more lasting impact. For a strong ending you can use several techniques, many of which resemble those used in the introduction.

- Show a broad application of the ideas suggested in the discussion.
- End with an authoritative direct quotation that reinforces your position.
- Challenge the reader.
- Echo the attention-getting sentences. For example, if you began with a direct quotation, you can refer to it again in the conclusion. This technique gives a nice circular structure to your discussion by bringing the thought-flow back around to where it began.

Applying Essay Techniques to Other Kinds of Writing

If you are answering an essay question on the CPA exam, you can use the techniques just discussed to organize and develop an effective discussion. But how do these techniques work with the writing formats more typically used by accountants—letters, memos, and reports?

First of all, everything you write should have a main idea. In an essay this idea is called the thesis statement; in a memo or report the main idea might be included in the statement of purpose (see Chapters 9 and 10). But whatever you're writing, it is a good idea to identify the main idea before you even begin your outline. Unless this idea is clear in your mind—or clearly written in your notes—what you write may be rambling and confusing. Your reader might then wonder, "What's this person trying to say? What's the point?"

So whatever you write should be organized around a central idea, just as an essay is organized. Letters, reports, and memos share other features of an essay as well: a basic three-part structure (introduction, body, conclusion); complex-deductive organization; and the need for adequate transitions and concrete support.

If you understand the principles discussed in this chapter, you will have an easier job planning and organizing the writing tasks which are part of your professional responsibilities.

SAMPLES OF ESSAYS

Below is an actual assignment for an essay in an intermediate accounting class. Following the assignment are two student answers that illustrate some of the principles of good organization and development.

ACCOUNTING 500
In-Class Paper I[2]

A small company has just hired you to replace its bookkeeper, who left for Barbados with a sales manager. Before the bookkeeper resigned, she explained the accounting system to the company president. In his fifteen-minute review of the system, the president learned his company had a general journal, four special journals, a general ledger, and two subsidiary ledgers.

His first suggestion to you is designed to cut cost and reduce duplication of effort. He suggests that you use only one journal instead of five and does not see any need for ledgers since they only duplicate what is already recorded in the journal.

Explain in 300–500 words how the president's suggestions may increase rather than reduce costs, and require more rather than less effort.

Essay 1[3]

Good accounting, like good management, relies on an organized system and a division of labor to reduce costs and minimize effort. Multiple journals and ledgers actually save the company time and money by isolating related accounts, delegating details, and summarizing information in controlling accounts. Isolation, delegation, and summarization free the accountant from the time-consuming task of sorting through overcrowded controlling accounts, thereby minimizing effort and reducing cost.

Isolation of accounts into special journals and subsidiary ledgers allows the accountant or manager to collect information on specific accounts in a small amount of time. Special journals, categorized as cash receipts, sales on account, purchases on account, and payments of cash, isolate each of these activities. Data can be reviewed for timely managerial decisions at a moment's notice because special journals eliminate the need to sort through other transactions. Likewise, subsidiary ledgers keep a running total of balances in a related category. The information remains separate and easily accessible and therefore of greatest use not only to the accountant, but also to management.

Delegation of transactions into special and subsidiary records eliminates clutter in controlling accounts and also allows for ease of data collection. For example, Herb Company has two thousand customers and over fifty creditors. The accountant uses subsidiary ledgers to organize these accounts into visible information. If a creditor double-bills the company, a quick check of that ledger will reveal the problem. Searching through a cluttered control account for the same information would prove tedious and leave room for error. Although subsidiary ledgers do require double posting, the initial expenditure of time more than repays itself in time and money saved. Those two thousand customers and over fifty creditors need room in subsidiary ledgers to free control accounts for other important transactions.

Finally, summarization of subsidiary and special records occurs in the controlling accounts, providing the accountant and management with an overall view of the company's transactions. Interested parties "get the big picture" without seeing all of the transactions at once because all account totals are posted to control accounts.

Cost reduction and labor savings result from the isolation, delegation, and summarization processes. Although account cutbacks may seem at first to provide an easy solution, after closer inspection the true picture emerges. Control accounts, supported by additional journals and ledgers, actually save time because of their unique organization, and that saves money.

Essay 2[4]

This company maintains an accounting system to record and summarize its economic activity, thereby helping management to make decisions. The system must be accurate to avoid misleading management; it must also be cost efficient. The company president suggests eliminating all special journals and any ledgers presently in use as a means "to cut cost and reduce duplication of effort" in the accounting system. This suggestion would not only increase personnel costs, but also increase errors.

This company's accounting system presently uses a double-entry system; that is, each transaction affects two accounts. Initially a transaction is recorded in a journal, either the general journal or a special journal. Journal entries are made daily, and all accounts affected by one transaction are listed in one place. This type of recording increases accuracy, because all debits and credits of one transaction are listed together and math errors can be spotted easily.

The special journals, such as cash receipts or cash payments journals, help categorize transactions. Entries in special journals are summarized at the end of each period, and only the totals in each account are posted to the ledger. This saves both time and effort; perhaps as many as fifty or sixty cash receipt journal entries per month may be summarized and posted to the ledger as one figure. The use of specialized journals saves posting time and allows transactions with common characteristics (sales, cash receipts) to be summarized.

The general ledger and subsidiary ledgers, much like special journals, summarize and classify accounting information. The ledger is a collection of all the company accounts. Journal entries are posted to the ledger accounts, and periodically ledger accounts are totaled, closed out to summary accounts if necessary, checked by a trial balance, and used to prepare financial statements. The ledger efficiently organizes and summarizes all information in the company journals. The subsidiary ledgers give more details about certain accounts. They facilitate looking up information about accounts receivable and accounts payable not consolidated in one place in the general ledger or general journal. Thus, both the ledger and the subsidiary ledgers efficiently summarize accounting data and serve as the primary sources of information for financial statements.

Eliminating special journals and all ledgers would probably decrease the accounting accuracy of this company and also increase costs, mostly in personnel time required to find and correct accounting errors and prepare financial statements.

Because one of the primary purposes of this accounting system is accurately to report and summarize economic activity, the advantages of special journals and ledgers outweight any disadvantages they may have.

NOTES

1. Steven C. Dabbs, "The Monetary Unit Assumption" (unpublished student paper, University of Georgia, 1976).
2. William Timothy O'Keefe, "Writing Assignment for Intermediate Accounting" (unpublished class assignment, University of Georgia, 1980).
3. Sandra L. Herbelin, "Journals and Ledgers" (unpublished student paper, University of Georgia, 1980).
4. Barbara Brown, "Journals and Ledgers" (unpublished student paper, University of Georgia, 1980).
5. Adapted from Charles Horngren, *Introduction to Financial Accounting* (Englewood Cliffs, N.J.: Prentice-Hall, Inc., © 1981), p. 65. Reprinted by permission.

EXERCISES

Discuss the topics defined in the following exercises, using the techniques covered in this and earlier chapters. Your answer might range from one to five paragraphs or more, depending on the topic.

Exercise 7-1 (Intermediate)
Contrast financial and managerial accounting.

Exercise 7-2 (Intermediate)
Define depreciation as used in accounting.

Exercise 7-3
(Intermediate)

The following are samples of the interpretations and remarks that are frequently encountered with regard to financial statements. Do you agree or disagree with these observations? Explain fully.

a. "Sales show the cash coming in from customers, and the various expenses show the cash going out for goods and services. The difference is net income."
b. "Why can't that big steel company pay higher wages and dividends too? It can use its hundreds of millions of dollars of retained income to do so."
c. "The total stockholders' equity measures the amount that the shareholders would get today if the corporation were liquidated."[5]

Exercise 7-4
(Intermediate)

Discuss why intraperiod tax allocation is necessary.

Exercise 7-5
(Intermediate)

Advocates of current value accounting propose several methods for determining the valuation of assets to approximate current values. Two of the methods proposed are replacement cost and present value of future cash flows.

Required:

Describe each of the two methods cited above and discuss the pros and cons of the various procedures used to arrive at the valuation for each method.*

Exercise 7-6
(Intermediate)

Inventory may be computed under one of various cost-flow assumptions. Among these assumptions are first-in, first-out (FIFO) and last-in, first-out (LIFO). In the past, some companies have changed from FIFO to LIFO for computing portions, or all, of their inventory.

Required:

1. Ignoring income tax, what effect does a change from FIFO to LIFO have on net earnings and working capital? Explain.
2. Explain the difference between the FIFO assumption of earnings and operating cycle and the LIFO assumption of earnings and operating cycle.**

Exercise 7-7
(Intermediate)

Generally accepted accounting principles require the use of accruals and deferrals in the determination of income.

Required:

a. How does accrual accounting affect the determination of income? Include in your discussion what constitutes an accrual and a deferral, and give appropriate examples of each.

*Material from Uniform CPA Examinations and Unofficial Answers, copyright © 1978 by the American Institute of Certified Public Accountants, Inc., is adapted with permission.

**Material from Uniform CPA Examinations and Unofficial Answers, copyright © 1979 by the American Institute of Certified Public Accountants, Inc., is adapted with permission.

b. Contrast accrual accounting with cash accounting.*

Exercise 7-8
(Intermediate)

The Financial Accounting Standards Board issued its Statement Number 12 to clarify accounting methods and procedures with respect to certain marketable securities. An important part of the statement concerns the distinction between noncurrent and current classification of marketable securities.

Required:

1. Why does a company maintain an investment portfolio of current and noncurrent securities?
2. What factors should be considered in determining whether investments in marketable equity securities should be classified as current or noncurrent, and how do these factors affect the accounting treatment for unrealized losses?**

Exercise 7-9
(Intermediate)

Financial accounting usually emphasizes the economic substance of events even though the legal form may differ and suggest different treatment. For example, under accrual accounting, expenses are recognized when they are incurred (substance) rather than when cash is disbursed (form).

Although the feature of substance over form exists in most generally accepted accounting principles and practices, there are times when form prevails over substance.

Required:

For each of the following topics, discuss the underlying theory in terms of both substance and form, i.e., substance over form and possibly form over substance in some cases. Each topic should be discussed independently.

a. Consolidated financial statements
b. Equity method of accounting for investments in common stock
c. Leases (including sale and leaseback)
d. Earnings per share (complex capital structure)***

Exercise 7-10 (Auditing)

Discuss the benefits of preparing an engagement letter.

Exercise 7-11 (Auditing)

The first generally accepted auditing standard of field work requires, in part, that "the work is to be adequately planned." An effective tool that aids the auditor in adequately planning the work is an audit program.

Required: Answer the following question in essay form.

What is an audit program, and what purposes does it serve?*

*Material from Uniform CPA Examinations and Unofficial Answers, copyright © 1977 by the American Institute of Certified Public Accountants, Inc., is adapted with permission.

Chapter 8

LETTERS

Accountants frequently need to write letters—to clients, government agencies, fellow professionals, and so on. They may write letters seeking data about a client's tax situation, for example, or information needed for an audit. They may also write letters to communicate the results of research into a technical accounting problem. Other typical letters written by accountants are engagement letters and management advisory letters.

For any letter to get the best results, of course, it must be well written.

This chapter will begin with some basic principles of good letter writing—organization, style, tone, and format. Then we will look at some of the typical kinds of letters accountants write.

BASIC PRINCIPLES OF LETTER WRITING

Effective letters have many of the characteristics of other good writing—tight organization, correct grammar and mechanics, conciseness, and an active, direct style. Letters should also be neat and attractive.

Begin with an Outline

Letters can vary in length from one paragraph to several pages, although many business letters are no longer than a page. But whatever the length, you should be certain about what you want to include before you begin; then you won't forget something important. In other words, jot down a brief outline of the ideas you want to cover before you begin to write. If you are answering another person's letter, have that letter before you, and make note of any comments for which a reply is needed.

Style and Tone: The You Attitude

One of the most important characteristics of a well-written business letter is its style and tone. Remember the six techniques for good style discussed in Chapter 5: simplicity, conciseness, concretion, variety, active voice, and precision. These rules apply as much to letters as to any other form of writing.

We can also look at the style and tone of business letters from another perspective—what many people call the "you attitude" in letter writing. Writers using this approach try to write from their correspondents' point of view, using the same courtesy and consideration shown in face-to-face communication. Actually, writing with the "you attitude" is similar to analyzing the readers' needs, a technique discussed in Chapter 2. But let's look at this approach as it applies more specifically to letters.

Courtesy.   First of all, the "you attitude" requires that you be courteous. Treat your correspondent with tact, politeness, and respect. Avoid abruptness, condescension, and stuffiness—or any other form of rudeness. Here are some examples of poor style in letter writing.

> This is a complicated subject, so I have tried to simplify it for you. (This sentence is condescending; it implies that the reader may not be very bright.)
>
> I acknowledge receipt of your letter and beg to thank you. (Too formal and artificial—stuffy, in fact.)
>
> Send me that report immediately. I can't understand why it has taken you so long to prepare it. (In certain situations you might *think* this way, but you'll get better results if you write with tact and courtesy.)

Pronouns.   Another technique in writing letters with the "you attitude" is to use personal pronouns. Use *you* and *I*, and in some situations, *we*. But avoid *we* when you really mean *I*.

> We have prepared the enclosed report on tax planning and hope that it will be helpful. If you have any further questions, please call on us. (This paragraph is fine if the report was actually prepared by more than one person. But if your name goes on the report's cover as its sole author, then use *I* rather than *we* in presenting it.)

Brevity and Clarity.   Brevity and clarity, qualities of all good writing, are particularly important in letters. You don't want to waste your readers' time, nor do you want them to miss your meaning. Come to the point quickly, and say it in a way they'll be sure to understand.

A number of the techniques already presented in this handbook are useful in achieving short, clear letters. For example, you will want your writing to be unified—paragraphs with a central idea that is easy to spot. You will also want the letter to be as concise and simple as possible, while still conveying an unambiguous, precise meaning.

Finally, when writing about a technical matter, analyze your readers' needs. Their knowledge and experience will determine how detailed the explanations should be. Sometimes, for example, you will need to explain complex, technical accounting procedures in words a nonaccountant could understand. Ray M. Sommerfeld and G. Fred Streuling, in their study *Tax Research Techniques,* have discussed user needs in writing letters to clients about tax problems:

> Like a good speaker, a good writer must know his audience before he begins. Because tax clients vary greatly in their own tax expertise, it is important to consider the technical sophistication of a client or his staff when composing a tax opinion letter. The style of a letter may range from a highly sophisticated format, which includes numerous technical explanations and citations, to a simple composition that utilizes only laymen's terms. In many situations, of course, the best solution lies somewhere between the two extremes.[1]*

Finally, remember that letters, like all the writing discussed in this handbook, should be precise.

Form and Appearance

One of the primary characteristics of an effective letter is a neat appearance. Good stationery is important: 8½ × 11-inch, unlined paper of a high-quality bond, about 24-pound weight. Envelopes, 4 × 10 inches, should match the stationery.

Business letters should be typed, using a typewriter and ribbon that will produce a neat, clear copy. If you must handwrite the letter, write legibly in black, blue, or blue-black ink. Corrections should be few and unobtrusive. Neatness is a must!

A letter is usually single spaced, with double spacing between paragraphs, although letters can be double spaced throughout (see the sample format on p. 94). Margins should be at least an inch on all sides and as even as possible, although the length of the letter will determine, in part, the margin width.

One-page letters should be placed so that the body of the letter, excluding the heading, is centered on the page or slightly above center. You may need to type a rough copy of the letter first and then adjust the size and placement of the margins to make them attractive.

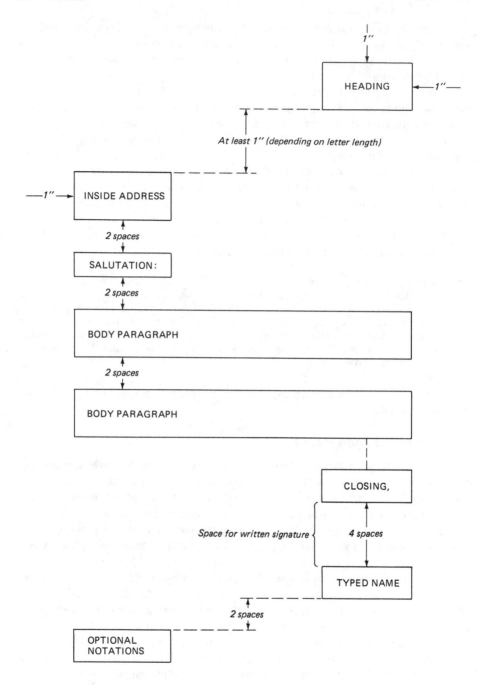

Most letters are written in the block or modified block style. The difference between the two styles is that paragraphs are indented in modified block style and not indented in block style. If you use block style, skip an extra line between paragraphs.

Study the diagram on page 94. This diagram identifies the parts of a letter and their proper placement.

Parts of the Letter

Heading.   The heading contains your address (not your name) and the date of the letter. If you use letterhead stationery, center the date under the printed heading or place it next to the right margin.

Inside Address.   The inside address is a reproduction of the address on the envelope. Place the title of the person to whom you are writing either on the same line as his or her name, or on the following line.

Anna M. Soper, President
Muffet Products
516 N. 25th Street
Athens, GA 30603

Anna M. Soper
Director of Personnel
Muffet Products
516 N. 25th Street
Athens, GA 30603

Note: Try to address a letter to a specific person, rather than to an office or title. You can often find the name of the person to whom you are writing by phoning the company or organization.

Salutation.   If possible, address your correspondent by name:

Dear Ms. Soper:
    or
Dear Mr. Smith:

For a woman correspondent, use *Ms.* if you don't know her marital status or if she prefers that title.

If you don't know the name of your correspondent, any of the following salutations is correct:

Dear Director of Personnel:
Dear Sir or Madam:
Dear Sir:
Dear Madam: } (If you know whether your correspondent is a man or woman.)

Note that a colon (:) always follows the salutation.

Body.   The body of a letter has three main parts:

1.   An introductory paragraph identifies the subject of the letter or the reason the letter was written. You may also need to identify previous correspondence on the subject.
2.   The message of the letter is divided into logical paragraphs.
3.   The concluding paragraph may be a formality: Thank you very much for your help in this matter.

The concluding paragraph is also a good place to tell your correspondent exactly what you want him or her to do:

May I have an appointment to discuss this matter with you? I'll be in Atlanta next week, October 7–12. I'll call your secretary to set up a time that is convenient for you.

Closing.   The formal closing of a letter, which usually is placed next to the right margin, comes immediately above the signature. Capitalize the first word, and put a comma after the closing. Any of the following closings is correct.

Sincerely yours,
Sincerely,
Yours very truly,
Very truly yours,

Signature.   Your name should be typed four spaces below the closing; your position can be typed beneath your name. The space between the closing and typed name is for your handwritten signature.

Sincerely,

Anna M. Soper

Anna M. Soper
President

Optional Parts of a Letter.   Sometimes you will need additional notations below the signature, on the left margin. First, if someone else types your letter, a notation is made of your initials (all capital letters) and the typist's (all lower case).

AMS:lc
   or
AMS/lc

Second, if the letter includes an enclosure, make a notation.

Enclosure(s)

Finally, if you will distribute copies of the letter to other people, note this fact.

cc: John Jones

Second Page.   Many business letters are only one page long. If you need to write additional pages, each one should have a heading identifying the addressee, the page number, and the date. This information is usually typed at the left margin.

Mr. Richard Smith
November 18, 19_____
Page 3

A Word about Layout

We have already said that a one-page letter should be positioned attractively on the page— with the bulk of it centered or slightly above center. With longer letters, layout may involve a few more considerations, especially the use of headings and set-off material.

If your letter covers several major topics, you can use headings to divide the letter into logical divisions. These divisions make the reader's job easier and enable him to see at a glance what your letter is about. Headings can be placed and typed in several ways; the sample letter on pages 101–102 shows one style. You can also find more information on headings in Chapter 10.

Another layout technique that sometimes makes letters more readable is set-off material, especially for enumerated lists. You can double space before and after the list and between entries, but single space each entry. Mark each item with a "bullet" or with numbers.

Example:
Your firm might use data processing equipment in at least five additional areas:

- budgets
- payrolls
- fixed assets
- accounts payable
- accounts receivable

The management advisory letter beginning on page 101 uses set-off material.

TYPICAL ACCOUNTING
LETTERS

Before we begin this section, we should note that many accounting firms have standardized letters for some situations. For example, the management of a firm may have decided on the organization and even the specific wording that it requires its staff to use for engagement letters, management advisory letters, and the like. If your firm uses standardized letters, you will simply adapt the basic letter to the specific case you are concerned with, adding dates, names, figures, and other relevant facts.

Presented below are sample letters for various situations, along with some general comments on the content and organization of these letters.

Engagement Letters

Engagement letters put into writing the arrangements made between an accounting firm and a client. Engagement letters can confirm the arrangements for a variety of services—audit, review, compilation, management advisory services, or tax. The main advantage of an engagement letter is that it clarifies the mutual responsibilities of accountant and client, and thus prevents possible misunderstandings.

Engagement letters can vary a great deal in content, depending on the firm writing the letter, the type of services to be provided, and the facts of the case. However, W. Peter Van Son, Dan M. Guy, and S. Frank Betts have identified three basic elements of most engagement letters:

- a description of the nature and limitations of the service that the accountants will provide
- a description of the reports that the accounting firm expects to issue
- a statement that the engagement will possibly not disclose errors, irregularities, or illegal acts[2]

In addition to these elements, an engagement letter may also include other information, such as important deadlines for the work; assistance that the client will provide, such as providing certain records and schedules; information about the fee; and a space for the client to indicate acceptance of the arrangements outlined in the engagement letter.

Page 99 shows a sample engagement letter for an audit.

Management Advisory
Letters

At the conclusion of an audit, an accountant often writes a letter to the client suggesting ways the client can improve the business. This type of letter may contain suggestions on a variety of topics. For example, the letter may include recommendations for improving

BROWN AND WYNNE
Certified Public Accountants

201 W. Tenth Street   Atlanta, Georgia 30315

July 15, 19XX

Mr. George Smith, President
Heritage Manufacturing Company
301 Planters Road
Athens, Georgia   30605

Dear Mr. Smith:

        This letter will confirm the arrangements we discussed for
the audit of Heritage Manufacturing Company for the year ended
December 31, 19XX.

        The purpose of the audit will be to examine Heritage
Company's financial statements for the year ended December 31,
19XX. Our examination will be conducted in accordance with
generally accepted auditing standards, and we will use the
tests and procedures necessary to express an opinion on the fair-
ness of the financial statements. As part of our audit, we will
review the internal control system and conduct tests of transactions. Although these procedures may disclose material errors
or illegal acts, a possibility remains that we may not dis-
cover irregularities during the course of the audit.

        At the close of our examination, we will issue our report
on the audit. We will also prepare your federal and state income
tax returns for the year ended December 31, 19XX. Both the audit
report and the tax returns should be complete about March 15,
19XX.

        Our fees will be at our regular rates, based on the time
required to perform these services. We will bill you when we
have completed the work.

        If you accept the arrangements outlined in this letter,
please indicate your acceptance by signing in the space below
and sending us the attached copy of this agreement.

        We are pleased that you have appointed us to be your audi-
tor, and we look forward to working with you and your staff.

                              Sincerely,

                              Carla Brown
                              Carla Brown, CPA

Accepted by:
Date:

- internal control
- the accounting and information system, including electronic data processing
- inventory control
- credit policies
- budgeting
- tax matters
- management of resources
- operating procedures

Sometimes, if the auditor includes many recommendations in the management letter, the letter may be quite long. If you write a management letter that is over three double-spaced, typed pages, organize it into a report with a transmittal letter (see Chapter 10). Address the transmittal letter to the president or board of directors of the client's company, and summarize in the letter the major recommendations made in the report.

In any case, whether the management letter is a single document or a report with a transmittal letter, remember that long letters are more attractive and easier to read if they contain headings. These headings will divide the letter into logical sections.

Whatever the format of your management letter, write it so that it will be helpful to your client and build a good professional relationship between the client and your firm. The techniques for effective writing discussed so far in this book are certainly applicable to management letters: clear and logical organization, readable style, and specific and concrete explanations.

In a recent article in the *Journal of Accountancy,* Robert T. Lanz and S. Thomas Moser noted that management letters often anger clients because the letters don't give enough specific information to support the accountants' suggestions.[3] Lanz and Moser stress the importance of answering three questions about each recommendation:

- Why is the change needed?
- How can it be accomplished?
- What benefits will the client receive?

In addition, Lanz and Moser note that the letter should be well organized, with key points summarized near the beginning. The authors conclude their article with a brief discussion about the style of management letters:

> Auditors may tend to write management letters in a perplexing combination of "legalese" and "accountantese." If this is what our clients are getting, we should put aside the technical jargon and verbosity and write a readable letter that makes good sense . . .[4]

An example of a short but effective management advisory letter appears on pages 101–102. The recommendations included in this letter are quoted from Lanz and Moser's article.[5]

BEASLEY AND POOLE
Certified Public Accountants
1553 W. Ellis Street
Atlanta, Georgia 30316

March 15, 19XX

Mr. Robert F. Freeman, President
Southeast Manufacturing Company
24 N. Broad Street
Atlanta, Georgia 30327

Dear Mr. Freeman:

Our examination of Southeast Manufacturing's financial statements for the year ending December 31, 19XX, revealed several areas where we believe you could improve your business:

· Adoption of data processing
· Stronger budgeting system
· Review of credit policies

The following paragraphs will explain these recommendations in greater detail.

Electronic Data Processing

Due to the large volume of paperwork processed and the complexity of related transactions, the present manual accounting system has become unwieldy. In this connection, we suggest that consideration be given to using data processing equipment in the following areas:
1. Sales
2. Budgets
3. Inventories
4. Accounts receivable and cash receipts
5. Accounts payable and cash disbursements
6. Payrolls
7. Fixed assets
8. General ledger and journal entries

Adoption of data processing in some or all of these areas would, we believe, reduce clerical workloads, tend to keep clerical salaries at a minimum and, most importantly, speed up bookkeeping functions in order to provide current financial information for management decisions and to facilitate the preparation of financial statements.

Budgets

Operating, selling and general and administrative expenses for 19X9 as compared with 19X8 increased from $1 million to $1,050,000, a change of 5 percent. Although management has been able to control expenditures, we believe efforts in this area would be assisted by implementation of a strong system of budgeting.

Under such a system, responsibility for actual performance is assigned to employees most directly responsible for the expenditures involved. (It is best that such employees have a role in establishing the budgets.) Periodic reports reflecting actual and budgeted amounts, together with explanations of significant variances, should be provided to management personnel responsible for approving the budgets initially. We cannot over-emphasize the value of sound budgeting and planning in all areas of the company's activities.

Credit Policies

The history of write-offs of bad accounts over the past few years indicates that the write-off percentage has declined. Considering the low net earnings margin under which the company operates (slightly less than .6 percent of net sales), it is most important that this favorable record continue since a significant increase in bad debts could have a substantial negative impact on net earnings.

In view of the high cost of money for business in general, management should consider reviewing its credit policies to reasonably assure that the risk inherent in continued sales to customers of questionable credit standing is justified. This is a delicate area of policy; it is not desirable to so restrict salesmen that profitable sales would be lost because of overly stringent credit policies. However, a reasonable amount of control should be exercised by the credit and collection department to assure a minimum of bad accounts. For example, a limit could be set on the amount which salesmen could extend to customers whose accounts have reached a certain balance.

We would be glad to discuss these suggestions with you and help you implement them.

Sincerely,

Roger Poole
Beasley and Poole
Certified Public Accountants

Tax Research Letters

Accountants who provide tax services must often write letters to their clients communicating the results of the research into some tax question. These letters can be for after-the-fact or tax planning situations.

The content and organization of these letters can vary, but Sommerfeld and Streuling suggest the following basic outline:[6]*

- the facts on which the research was based
- warning that the advice is valid only for the facts previously outlined
- the tax questions implicit in these facts
- the conclusions, with the authoritative support for the conclusions
- areas of controversy that the IRS might dispute (Tax accountants do not all agree that the letter should identify the vulnerable areas in the client's situation. Sommerfeld and Streuling suggest that if the letter does identify these weaknesses, the accountant should caution the client to control access to the letter.)

In addition to a logical organization, such as the one outlined here, it is important that tax research letters be understandable to the client. Tax questions are often highly technical, and the accountant may need to explain the conclusions in terms a business person will understand. Read again the quotation at the beginning of the chapter that emphasizes the importance of writing with specific readers in mind.

A sample letter reporting the results of tax research appears on pages 104–106.[7]**

NOTES

1. Ray M. Sommerfeld and G. Fred Streuling, *Tax Research Techniques*, Studies in Federal Taxation No. 5 (New York: American Institute of Certified Public Accountants, 1976), p. 166.

    Sommerfeld and Streuling give additional information on other letters that tax accountants sometimes write: tax protest letters, requests for rulings, and determination letters.
2. W. Peter Van Son, Dan M. Guy, and J. Frank Betts, "Engagement Letters: What Practice Shows," *Journal of Accountancy*, 152, no. 6 (June 1982), p. 76.
3. Robert T. Lanz and S. Thomas Moser, "Improving Management Letters," *Journal of Accountancy*, 149, no. 3 (March 1980), pp. 39–42.
4. Lanz and Moser, "Management Letters," p. 42.
5. Lanz and Moser, "Management Letters," pp. 41–42.
6. Sommerfeld and Streuling, *Tax Research Techniques*, pp. 166–69.
7. Sommerfeld and Streuling, *Tax Research Techniques*, pp. 183–85.
8. Malcolm H. Lathan, "Writing Assignment for Intermediate Accounting" (unpublished class assignment, University of Georgia, 1982).

ROBERT U. PARTNER & COMPANY
Certified Public Accountants
2010 Professional Tower
Calum City, U.S.A. 00001

December 23, 19X5

Mr. Red E. Ink, President
Ready, Incorporated
120 Publisher Lane
Calum City, USA 00002

Dear Mr. Ink:

This letter confirms the oral agreement of December 17,
19X5, in which our firm agreed to undertake the preparation of
federal income tax returns for you and Ready, Inc., for the next
year. The letter also reports the preliminary results of our
investigation into the tax consequences of the incorporation of
your printing business last March. We are pleased to be of service to you and anticipate that our relationship will prove to
be mutually beneficial. Please feel free to call upon me at any
time.

Before stating the preliminary results of our investigation
into the tax consequences of your incorporation transaction, I
would like to restate briefly all of the important facts as
we understand them. Please review this statement of facts very
carefully. Our conclusions depend upon a complete and accurate
understanding of all of the facts. If any of the following
statements is either incorrect or incomplete, please call it to
my attention immediately, no matter how small or insignificant
the difference may appear to be.

Our conclusions are based upon an understanding that on
March 1, 19X5, you exchanged all of the assets and liabilities of
the printing business, which you had operated for the prior
twelve years as a sole proprietorship, for 1,000 shares of common
stock in Ready, Inc., a newly formed corporation. The assets
that you transferred to Ready, Inc., consisted of $20,000 cash;
$10,000 (estimated market value) supplies on hand; $50,000 (face
value) trade receivables; and $60,000 (book value) equipment.
The equipment, purchased new in 19X1 for $100,000, had been
depreciated on a double-declining-balance method for the past
four years. An investment credit was claimed in 19X1 on the purchase of the equipment. The liabilities assumed by Ready, Inc.,
consisted of the $40,000 mortgage remaining from the original
equipment purchase in 19X1 and current trade payables of $10,000.
We further understand that Ready, Inc., plans to continue to
occupy the building leased by you on October 1, 19X3, from
Branden Properties, until the expiration of that lease on
September 30, 19X7. Finally, we understand that Ready, Inc.,

has issued only 1,000 shares of common stock and that you retain
980 of those shares; that your wife, Neva, holds ten shares; and
that Tom Books, the corporate secretary-treasurer, holds the
remaining ten shares. The shares held by Mrs. Ink and Mr. Books
were given to them by you, as a gift, on March 1, 19X5.

Assuming that the preceding paragraph represents a complete
and accurate statement of all of the facts pertinent to your
incorporation transaction, we anticipate reporting that event as
a wholly nontaxable transaction. In other words, neither you
(individually) nor your corporation will report any taxable
income or loss solely because of your incorporation of the printing business. Furthermore, no amount of investment credit will
have to be recaptured. However, in the future Ready, Inc. will
be restricted to a 150 percent declining-balance depreciation
deduction on the equipment transferred. The trade receivables
collected by Ready, Inc., after March 1, 19X5, will be reported
as the taxable income of the corporate entity; collections made
between January 1, 19X5, and February 28, 19X5, will be considered part of your personal taxable income for 19X5.

If Ready, Inc.'s tax return is audited, there is a possibility that the Internal Revenue Service may challenge the corporation's right to deduct the $10,000 in trade payables it assumed
from your proprietorship. If you so desire, I would be pleased
to explain this matter in detail. Perhaps it would be desirable
for Mr. Bent, you, and me to meet and review this potential problem prior to our filing the corporate tax return.

If you wish to report the first corporate taxable income on
a cash-method fiscal-year basis, ending February 29, 19X6, it is
imperative that you have Mr. Tom Books keep the corporation's
regular financial accounts on that same basis. If he desires any
help in maintaining those records, we will be happy to assist
him. It will be necessary for us to have access to your personal
financial records no later than March 1, 19X5, and to your corporate records no later than April 15, 19X5, if the two federal
income tax returns are to be completed and filed on a timely
basis.

Finally, may I suggest that we plan to have at least one
more meeting in my office sometime prior to February 28, 19X6,
to discuss possible tax-planning opportunities available to you
in the new corporation. Among other considerations, we should
jointly review the possibility that you may want to make a Sub-
chapter S election, and that you may need to structure executive
compensation arrangements carefully and may wish to institute a
pension plan. It may be desirable to discuss these opportunities

Red E. Ink
December 23, 19X5
Page 3

at the same time that we meet with Mr. Bent to consider the
question of deducting the $10,000 in trade payables, as noted
earlier. Please telephone me to arrange an appointment if you
would like to do this shortly after the holidays.

Thank you again for selecting our firm for tax assistance.
It is very important that some of the material in this letter
be kept confidential, and we strongly recommend that you carefully control access to it at all times. If you have any questions about any of the matters discussed, feel free to request
a more detailed explanation or drop by and review the complete
files, which are available in my office. If I should not be
available, my assistant, Fred Senior, would be happy to help you.
We look forward to serving you in the future.

Sincerely yours,

Robert U. Partner

9. Randolph A. Shockley, "Writing Assignment for Intermediate Accounting" (unpublished class assignment, University of Georgia, 1982).

10. Charles Horngren, *Introduction to Financial Accounting* (Englewood Cliffs, N.J.: Prentice-Hall, Inc., © 1981), p. 72. Reprinted by permission.

11. Adapted from Howard F. Stettler, *Auditing Principles: A Systems-Based Approach* (Englewood Cliffs, N.J.: Prentice-Hall, Inc., © 1982), pp. 667–68. Reprinted by permission.

EXERCISES

Write letters for the situations described below. Use the proper format and effective organization and style. Invent any information you feel is necessary to make your letters complete.

Exercise 8-1 (all levels)

You are considering a move to a distant city, and you would like to work with a local accounting firm there. You have five years' experience working as a CPA in the city where you now live.

Write a letter requesting an interview to discuss possible employment with the firm for which you wish to work.

Exercise 8-2 (all levels)

You have prepared the federal and state income tax returns for your client, Alexander Littleton. Write a cover letter to Mr. Littleton to mail with the completed returns. In your letter include:

*   a reminder for him to sign the returns on the lines checked
*   the amounts that he owes in both state and federal taxes
*   a reminder of the filing deadline

Exercise 8-3 (all levels)

One of your clients, Alan Motors, has not paid for an audit that you completed March 15, 19XX. You billed Alan at the time you completed the audit, and mailed a reminder in May. At the end of June, Alan still hasn't paid the bill, and you need to write a letter to the company president, Mr. Roger Alan, requesting payment. Of course you don't want to antagonize Mr. Alan, because the company has been a client for several years and you value the business relationship.

Write the letter to Mr. Alan asking him to pay the bill.

Exercise 8-4 (all levels)

You are preparing the federal income tax returns for Mr. and Mrs. John Lapp and find you need some additional information: receipts for contributions to their church, the name of their youngest child, and the name of the day care center where the child is enrolled.

Write a letter to Mr. and Mrs. Lapp requesting this information.

Exercise 8-5
(Intermediate)

A friend of yours, Debbie Debit, has written you for advice. She tells you that she owns several shares of stock in Alpha Corporation. She has examined the most recent balance sheet of Alpha and has found that the common stock issued and outstanding totals 40,000 shares, and the market price per share is $25 on the balance sheet date. She is sure that the balance sheet is in error because, in her words, "the total assets are $1,100,000 and this current value should be the same as the total market value of the outstanding common stock."

Required:

In a letter, explain to your friend the various classifications of assets and how the "value" of each classification is determined to derive the "value" of the $1,100,000 in total assets. Also explain why the "values" of the assets and the stock are not the same.[8]

Exercise 8-6
(Intermediate)

One morning J. Worthington Pocketmoney stormed into the offices of Apple, Altos, and Monroe, his certified public accountants. Without waiting for the receptionist to announce his arrival, he entered the office of Samuel Andrews, the partner in charge of auditing Mr. Pocketmoney's home appliance store. As usual, Mr. Andrews listened politely and calmly to the monologue delivered by Mr. Pocketmoney. An edited version follows.

> This morning at my breakfast club I spoke with my competitor, F. Scott Wurlitzer. He boasted that his accountant had saved him $19,000 in income taxes last year by recommending a switch from the FIFO to the LIFO inventory flow assumption. If he can do that, why can't I? And why haven't you discussed this gimmick with me? I don't expect to rely on Wurlitzer for financial advice; I pay you for that.

After Pocketmoney's departure, Mr. Andrews calls you, a new staff accountant, into his office. He expresses regret at not having mentioned to Pocketmoney the possibility of a change in accounting principle. However, he also advises you that Pocketmoney needs new capital in his business and is trying to interest another local businessperson in becoming a limited partner. Thus a decline in reported income could be detrimental to Mr. Pocketmoney's plans.

Mr. Andrews assigns you to draft a letter to Mr. Pocketmoney. The letter should provide a balanced discussion of the advantages and disadvantages of shifting from FIFO to LIFO, with particular reference to Mr. Pocketmoney's specific situation. Even though Andrews would like to provide some justification for his firm's failure to mention the possibility of a change, he cautions you to be reasonably objective and give adequate consideration to accounting theory.[9]

Exercise 8-7
(Intermediate)

Joel Barlow, the president of Marvel Cars, Inc., has sent you his firm's income statement, which is shown below. He has asked you to evaluate the statement and tell him of any shortcomings you find.

Write a letter to Mr. Barlow in which you discuss the problems you find with his firm's income statement.[10]

MARVEL CARS, INC.
Statement of Profit and Loss
December 31, 19X3

Revenues:		
Sales	$1,000,000	
Increase in market value of land and building	200,000	$1,200,000
Deduct expenses:		
Advertising	$100,000	
Sales commissions	50,000	
Utilities	20,000	
Wages	150,000	
Dividends	100,000	
Cost of cars purchased	700,000	1,120,000
Net profit		$ 80,000

Excroise 8-8
(Intermediate)

Mr. and Mrs. Richard Webster want to invest in a deferred annuity for their son, Charles, who is ten years old. They want the annuity to pay exactly $10,000 a year for five years, beginning when Charles turns twenty-one. They want to know how much money they will have to invest now, assuming the money will earn interest, compounded annually, of 14 percent.

Write a letter to Mr. and Mrs. Webster explaining deferred annuities and the amount they would need to invest now to set up the plan they have in mind.

Exercise 8-9 (Auditing)

Write an engagement letter in which you agree to review the financial statements of Howard Fabricators, Inc. You may mention other services that you agree to provide.

Exercise 8-10 (Auditing)

One of your audit clients is Brown Manufacturing, which is owned by Charles Brown. Although your client has not discussed the problem with you, you have concluded that the business is in dire need of additional liquid funds. You have noted that payables are being liquidated well after discount dates have expired and that most equipment is being leased, rather than being purchased as is customary in most businesses of this type. The problem is being aggravated by a continued comfortable increase in volume, which has necessitated carrying larger inventories and receivables and leasing additional equipment at rates well in excess of normal depreciation charges and interest. The owner of the business has already invested all his available liquid funds in the business.[11]

Write a letter to Mr. Brown, suggesting ways he could improve the liquidity of his business.

Exercise 8-11 (Cost)

Everett Yale, president of Hotchkiss, Inc., your client, recently attended a seminar at which a speaker discussed planning and control of capital expenditures. The speaker referred to this approach as "capital budgeting." Yale tells you that he is not quite sure he understands this concept.

Required:

a. Explain the nature and identify several uses of capital budgeting.
b. What are the basic differences between the payback (payout) method and the net present value method of capital budgeting? Explain.
c. Define "cost of capital."
d. Financial accounting data are not entirely suitable for use in capital budgeting. Explain.

Write a letter to Mr. Yale in which you answer his questions.*

Exercise 8-12 (Auditing)

You have examined the financial statements of the Broadwall Corporation, a publicly held company, for the year ended December 31, 19X1. Jack Elliot, President of Broadwall, has asked you to perform a limited review of the corporation's statements for the period ending March 31, 19X2.

Write a letter to Mr. Elliot. Explain why your limited review will not provide a basis for the expression of an opinion.**

---

*Material from Uniform CPA Examinations and Unofficial Answers, copyright © 1977 by the American Institute of Certified Public Accountants, Inc., is adapted with permission.

**Material from Uniform CPA Examinations and Unofficial Answers, copyright © 1979 by the American Institute of Certified Public Accountants, Inc., is adapted with permission.

Chapter 9

MEMORANDUMS

Memorandums are used for communication within an organization—between departments, for example, or between supervisor and staff. Memos may be of any length, from one sentence to several pages. They are usually less formal than letters written to people outside the organization, but well-written memos have the same qualities as good letters: clarity, brevity, and courtesy—all the techniques of the "you attitude" (see Chapter 8).

This chapter will first discuss some of the general characteristics of effective memos. Then we will look at two special kinds of memos that accountants often write: memos to clients' files and memos that are part of working papers.

MEMORANDUMS: SOME
BASIC COMMENTS

Frequently memos are quite short—from one sentence, perhaps, to several paragraphs. Here is an example:

MEMORANDUM   June 5, 19XX

To: All department heads

From: John Moore

Subject: ENERGY CONSERVATION

As you know, our firm has recently begun a program of energy conservation. Therefore, please set your thermostats for the summer at 78 degrees and turn off all the lights when you close your office for the day.

Thank you for your cooperation.

Notice the heading of the memo: the date, the person or persons addressed, the writer, and the subject. Frequently, as in this example, the writer's initials replace a formal signature.

Sometimes memos may be much longer than this one; in fact, they may be used for short reports. For longer memos, organization and structure are more complicated. A long memo needs a brief introduction that identifies the subject of the memo and refers to the situation for which it was written. Following the introduction should be a short summary of the memo's main ideas, including any appropriate recommendations. The body of a longer memo should be divided into sections, with appropriate headings; it should end with a brief conclusion. Introductions, initial summaries, and headings are explained more thoroughly in the chapter that deals with reports.

Effective memos, like all forms of good writing, illustrate the techniques for effective writing discussed in earlier chapters:

- analysis of purpose and readers' needs
- logical organization, including transitions
- readable style, including active voice, simplicity, conciseness, and concretion
- precision
- correct grammar and mechanics

Below is a situation that required a memorandum, and the memo that resulted. (The memo in this example contains documentation and a bibliography because it was written for a class assignment requiring documented research. Memos do not usually show formal documentation.)

Situation:[1]

Your client found three suitable sites, each having certain unique advantages, for a new plant facility. In order to investigate thoroughly the advantages and disadvantages of each site, your client purchased one-year options for an amount equal to 5% of the contract price of each site. The costs of the options cannot be applied against the contract prices. Before the options expired, the client purchased one of the sites at the contract price of $60,000. The option on this site had cost $3,000. The two options not exercised had cost $3,500 each.

The controller is uncertain of the total cost to be capitalized under GAAP. The partner in charge of the audit has asked you to draft a memo presenting arguments in support of recording the cost of the land at 1) $60,000, 2) $63,000, and 3) $70,000. The memo is also to include your recommendation for a specific amount to be capitalized, and a specific rationale for your decision.

May 3, 19XX

MEMORANDUM[2]
To: R. A. Shockley, Partner
FROM: Jane Paustian, Staff Accountant
SUBJECT: Recording Land Option Costs for Smith Company

Accountants are sometimes uncertain about which costs a business enterprise should include in the purchase of land. For the Smith Company, a question arises as to whether its accountants should include the $3,000 exercised land option and the two $3,500 options not exercised in the cost of a $60,000 tract of land. This memo will recommend a specific amount for Smith Co. to capitalize by first examining the rules for recording costs under Generally Accepted Accounting Principles. The memo will then review three alternative methods of recording the land options' costs, which include capitalizing all three options, expensing all three options, or capitalizing the exercised option only.

Initial Summary and Recommendation

Smith Company can best evaluate the three available alternatives for recording the option costs by examining both Accounting Principles Board Statement No. 4 and Financial Accounting Standards Board Statement No. 3. These pronouncements state that an entity may capitalize only those costs that provide a future economic benefit to the firm. From this definition, one can formulate good arguments in favor of capitalizing all three options or expensing all three options. However, the most appropriate method is for the Smith Company to view the three options separately. Since the exercised option provides a future benefit of a land acquisition, Smith Company should capitalize the cost of this option as part of the cost of the land. However, the two options on the alternative parcels of land will expire and thus produce no future benefit. Therefore, Smith Company should expense these option costs when they expire.

Recording Costs

Generally Accepted Accounting Principles provide criteria for Smith Company to evaluate the different alternatives for recording the options' costs. According to Financial Accounting Standards Board Statement No. 3, if a cost provides future economic benefit that can be controlled by the entity, and the transaction that gives rise to that control has already occurred, the entity should capitalize that cost in an asset account and expense it over the asset's useful life. On the other hand, Accounting Principles Board Statement No. 4 states that if a cost provides no future benefit to the entity, the entity should simply expense it in the period in which it is incurred.

From these basic rules for recording costs, we will examine how to record the costs of the land options in question.

Capitalize All Options

The first method of recording the costs of the land options is to capitalize all three options purchased. As stated above, capitalization of costs requires that the costs provide future economic benefits and that transactions giving rise to those benefits have already occurred. Obviously, the future benefit of purchased land options is the parcel of land that the Smith Co. will eventually purchase. Not only did the option on the purchased land parcel lead to the decision to acquire the land, but the two options on the alternative parcels of land also led to the decision. Also, the transactions giving rise to the future benefit occurred when the Smith Co. purchased the land options. Therefore, the option costs meet the two criteria for capitalization.

Furthermore, Edwards, Johnson, and Roemmich specifically state that "the cost of land includes any current cash outlay, or a commitment for a future cash outlay, which is incurred to get the land ready for use in its intended purpose."[1] Because the Smith Co. purchased *all three* options in order to acquire one parcel of land, the options' costs were costs of getting the land ready for use. Therefore, the Smith Co. could capitalize the costs of all three options. The balance in the Land account would then include the $60,000 contract price, as well as the $3,000 exercised option and the two $3,500 options not exercised.

Expense All Options

Although Edwards, Johnson, and Roemmich state that an entity should capitalize all costs *incurred* to get the land ready for use, some accountants believe that the entity should capitalize only those expenditures *necessary* to place the land in readiness for use. The question of whether any of the options were *necessary* to acquire the land is a difficult one. Smith Co. could have foregone the purchase of any options and simply taken its time to investigate each site. Although there would have been a risk of losing the land to another buyer, Smith Co. could still have purchased the land without purchasing any options. Therefore, since uncertainties exist as to whether the options themselves are necessary for providing future benefit, Smith Co. should, under both A.P.B. #4 and the conservatism principle, expense the costs of all three options in the period in which they were incurred. This will result in a $60,000 balance in the Land account, that of the contract price only.

Capitalize Only the
Exercised Option

Since the methods above are quite different and yet are both supported by Generally Accepted Accounting Principles, it would seem that the "best" method would be a compromise between the two. The most logical approach to determining how to record the three options is to view them separately. Although all three options led to Smith Co.'s decision to buy one particular land tract, only the exercised option actually provided for the purchase of that land. Therefore, *only* the exercised option provides for a future economic benefit, and so Smith Co. should capitalize it as a cost of getting the land in readiness for use. The other two options result in no purchase of their respective land tracts and thus will expire and provide no future benefit to the enterprise. Therefore, Smith Co. should expense these costs when they expire. Thus, the resulting balance in the Land account will be $63,000 and will consist of the $60,000 contract price and the $3,000 exercised option.

Conclusion

We have examined several methods for the Smith Co. to record the costs of the three land options purchased. Although application of the rules for recording costs can conceivably result in capitalizing or expensing all three options, the most appropriate method is for Smith Co. to apply the rules to each option. Such an application results in Smith Co.'s capitalizing the exercised option and expensing the two other options. Smith Co. will then reflect in its Land account only those costs that actually provide a future benefit for the certain tract of land. Likewise, Smith Co. will adhere to the conservatism principle by expensing those costs which do not directly benefit the land actually purchased.

Note

1.   James D. Edwards, Johnny R. Johnson, and Roger A. Roemmich, *Intermediate Accounting* (Plano, Texas: Business Publications, Inc., 1981), p. 307.

Bibliography

ACCOUNTING PRINCIPLES BOARD.   *Basic Concepts and Accounting Principles Underlying Financial Statements of Business Enterprises.* Statement of the Accounting Principles Board No. 4. Rpt. in American Institute of Certified Public Accountants. *Professional Standards.* Vol. III: *Accounting: Current Text.* Chicago: Commerce Clearing House, Inc., 1978.
EDWARDS, JAMES D., JOHNSON, JOHNNY R., AND ROEMMICH, ROGER A.   *Intermediate Accounting.* Plano, Texas. Business Publications, Inc., 1981.
FINANCIAL ACCOUNTING STANDARDS BOARD.   *Elements of Financial Statements of Business Enterprises.* Statement of Financial Accounting Concepts No. 3. Rpt. in American Institute of Certified Public Accountants. *Professional Standards.* Vol. III: *Accounting: Current Text.* Chicago: Commerce Clearing House, Inc., 1978.

MEMOS TO CLIENTS' FILES

Sometimes accountants record information about a client's situation in a memorandum that is placed in the client's file for later reference. Other members of the staff may refer to the information recorded in these memos months or even years later, so it is important that the information be recorded clearly, accurately, and correctly.

For example, a client may write or call an accounting firm about a tax question. The person receiving the letter or handling the call will then write a memo to record the pertinent facts of the client's situation. Later, another member of the staff can research the question. The researcher will need adequate information to

identify the issues, locate appropriate literature, and solve the client's problem.[3]*
Below is a sample of a memo written for a client's file[4]**

October 30, 19XX

TO: Files

FROM: Tom Partner T.P.

SUBJECT: Potential exchange of common voting stock for preferred nonvoting stock in Allemania Electronic, Inc.

Today, Tim Dietz, financial vice-president of Electric Supply Co., called to request information concerning the tax consequences of a proposed recapitalization in Allemania Electronic, Inc., an 85-percent-owned subsidiary.

Allemania was acquired by Electric on June 1, 19X1, and has been carried in the financial statements as a temporary investment on the equity basis. The auditors of Electric (Meyerson, Garner, and Leavitt) are now insisting that continued association with Allemania would require the inclusion of the subsidiary in Electric's financial statements on a fully consolidated basis. The directors of Allemania are not in favor of such a disclosure and have suggested that Allemania exchange sufficient common voting stock for preferred nonvoting stock to reduce Electric's ownership in the form of voting stock from 85 percent to 50 percent or below. The board hopes, through the reduction of ownership in voting stock, that inclusion of Allemania on a consolidated financial basis with Electric can be avoided.

At the present time Electric and Allemania join in the filing of a consolidated tax return on a May 31, fiscal-year basis. Responsibility for preparation and filing of the return rests with Electric's internal tax department, which we review on an annual basis.

Tim Dietz requested that our report reach him prior to Electric's next board meeting, which is scheduled for November 22, and he requested that we contact him personally for additional information.

MEMOS AS PART OF
WORKING PAPERS

When accountants prepare working papers as part of their work on a case, they usually include memorandums summarizing the work they have performed, what they have observed, and the conclusions they have reached. In an audit, for example, the audit staff members prepare memos describing each major area of the audit. Then a supervisor, perhaps the auditor in charge or the engagement partner, will often prepare a summary or review memo that includes comments on the entire audit process.

It is important that these memos be clear, accurate, and complete. Other members of the firm, or lawyers on either side of a court case who review the working papers later, may need to know exactly what procedures the auditors performed. Thus, these memos should be written in a direct, active style: "I [the person writing the memo] performed a cash receipts walk-through on May 31, 19XX. I used admission ticket #51065 for the test."

Below is a memorandum written to record an inventory observation.[5]

Prepared by: C.J.G. Date: 1/5/X2
Reviewed by: A.C.E. Date: 1/11/X2

Highlight Company   F-3
Inventory Observation Memorandum—Wayne Plant A
12/31/X1

1. *Observing clients' inventory taking.* Four members of our audit staff arrived at the Wayne Plant at 7:40 A.M. on 12/31/X1 for the inventory observation. All manufacturing and shipping operations had been shut down for the day. All materials had been neatly arranged, labeled, and separated by type.

    Two teams of audit staff members each were assigned to different parts of the plant. Each team observed the care with which the client's personnel made the inventory counts and the control being exercised over the inventory count sheets. In every case, it appeared that the client's inventory instructions were being followed in a systematic and conscientious manner.

2. *Making test counts.* Each team made numerous test counts, which were recorded in our work papers (see F-2). The test counts covered approximately 22 percent of the inventory value and confirmed the accuracy of the client's counts.

3. *Identifying obsolete and damaged goods.* Each team made inquiries concerning obsolete, damaged, or slow-moving items. Based on our observations and inquiries, we have no reason to believe that any obsolete or damaged materials remained in inventory. We identified certain slow-moving items, portions of which on further investigation were excluded from the inventory (see F-4).

4. *Observing cutoff controls.* We observed that receiving reports were prepared on all goods received on the inventory date and recorded the number of the last receiving report prepared. No goods were shipped on 12/31. We recorded the number of the last shipping document used on 12/30. These numbers were subsequently used in our purchases and sales cutoff tests (see F-6 and F-7).

5. *Conclusions.* Based on our observation of the procedures followed by the client, it is my opinion that an accurate count was made of all goods on hand at 12/31/X1 and that all obsolete, damaged, or slow-moving items were appropriately identified.

Carl Good   C.G.

Notes

1. Adapted from A. N. Mosich and E. John Larsen, *Intermediate Accounting,* 5th edition (New York: McGraw-Hill Book Company, 1982), p. 473.

2. Jane Paustian, "Recording Land Option Costs for Smith Company" (unpublished student paper, University of Georgia, 1982).

3. Ray M. Sommerfeld and G. Fred Streuling, *Tax Research Techniques,* Studies in

Federal Taxation No. 5 (New York: American Institute of Certified Public Accountants, 1976), p. 162.

4. Adapted from Sommerfeld and Streuling, *Tax Research Techniques,* p. 163.

5. Reprinted, by permission, from pp. 490–491 in *Modern Auditing* by Walter G. Kell and Richard E. Ziegler. Copyright © 1980 by John Wiley & Sons, Inc.

6. William Timothy O'Keefe, "Writing Assignment for Intermediate Accounting" (unpublished class assignment, University of Georgia, 1980).

7. Malcolm H. Lathan, "Writing Assignment for Intermediate Accounting" (unpublished class assignment, University of Georgia, 1982).

8. Ibid.

9. Gadis J. Dillon, "Writing Assignment for Intermediate Accounting" (unpublished class assignment, University of Georgia, 1982).

10. Ibid.

11. Gordon S. May, "Writing Assignment for Intermediate Accounting" (unpublished class assignment, University of Georgia, 1982).

12. Charles T. Horngren, *Introduction to Financial Accounting* (Englewood Cliffs, N.J.: Prentice-Hall, Inc., © 1981), p. 336. Reprinted by permission.

13. Charles T. Horngren, *Introduction to Management Accounting,* 5th edition (Englewood Cliffs, N.J.: Prentice-Hall, Inc., © 1981), p. 110. Reprinted by permission.

14. Alvin A. Arens and James K. Loebbecke, *Auditing: An Integrated Approach,* 2nd edition (Englewood Cliffs, N.J.: Prentice-Hall, Inc., © 1980), p. 170. Reprinted by permission.

15. Ibid., p. 209.

EXERCISES

For the following situations, write the memorandums required. Invent any details you need, such as names of firms and individuals.

Exercise 9-1
(Intermediate)

You have just been hired to join the accounting staff of Dirty McNasty, Inc. As the controller of the firm, Joyce Moore, is welcoming you in her office on your first day, Mr. McNasty, the president of the company, walks in. After introductions and pleasantries, the president turns to the controller: "Joyce, you know I have little knowledge about accounting, but it seems inefficient to me to have five different journals in this company. It increases the amount of accounting work we must do and increases the chance of errors. Wouldn't it be more reasonable to have one journal? Give me your thoughts on the matter in a short note whenever you get the time."

The controller explains that when Old Dirty says ". . . whenever you get the time," he means, ". . . make time, now." She is about to cancel her plans for the evening when you seize the opportunity to make a good impression and earn points with the boss. You offer to stay late and write the memo for the controller, promising to do a great job. She accepts your offer.

Required:
    Prepare in good form a memorandum that explains why it is efficient to use the following journals:

- Cash Disbursements Journal
- Cash Receipts Journal
- Sales Journal
- Purchases Journal
- General Journal

    Address the memo to the president from the controller. Remember that the president has very little accounting knowledge.[6]

Exercise 9-2
(Intermediate)

    You are employed as a special assistant to Mr. Joseph Anderson, president of Bulldog Sales Company. Mr. Anderson has just received the monthly financial statements for the company from the controller. After reviewing them with you, he says, "You know, the results of these statements bother me. We show net earnings of $150,000 for last month, but the balance sheet shows the value of the company at about the same amount as last year. You know the value of the company is much more now."

    "You're probably right," you reply. "But there are certain factors and rules in accounting that sometimes prevent reported operating results from reflecting the change in real value of the company."

Required:
    Prepare in good form a memorandum that clearly explains the reasons financial statements do not necessarily reflect the economic value of a company. The memorandum should be addressed to Mr. Anderson.[7]

Exercise 9-3
(Intermediate)

    A friend of yours, Carl Credit, has come to you for advice. He has received an entry to the most recent Consumers Sweepstakes. He is puzzled over the prizes and the options available to him. A summary of the prizes follows:

Grand Prize:	$125,000 Cash
	or
	$ 20,000 per year for 10 years
First Prize:	$100,000 Cash
	or
	$ 24,000 per year for 6 years

Second Prize:	$ 80,000 Cash
	or
	$ 20,000 per year for 5 years
Third Prize:	$ 60,000 Cash
	or
	$ 18,000 per year for 4 years

Carl knows that he will receive more total cash if he selects the periodic payments for each of the prizes, but he is afraid that he is "missing" something in the offer (he does not understand present value principles).

Required:

In a memorandum, explain to Carl the time value of money. Also, advise him which settlement option for each of the prizes is better. (Carl must select the settlement options before submitting his entry.) Assume that payments are made at the beginning of each year and compute the interest rate at which Carl would be indifferent between the options. (You may present your calculations as a supporting exhibit to your memo and you may ignore income taxes.)[8]

Exercise 9-4
(Intermediate)

You have been hired as a special assistant to Sam Jones, the president of Bulldog Sales Company. Mr. Jones has little formal education, but is very astute about business matters and is an especially good salesperson. He calls you in and says, "Bulldog Sales Company is in the nice position of having excess cash on hand. I am considering investing that cash in some bonds issued in 1975 by Red and Black Company, but I see in the *Wall Street Journal* that those bonds are selling at only 60% of their maturity value. Does that mean they are especially risky? Assuming I do make this investment, what are the accounting implications?"

Write a memorandum answering Mr. Jones's questions.[9]

Exercise 9-5
(Intermediate)

You are manager of the accounting department of Greenwood Sales Company, reporting directly to John Wilson, president. Mr. Wilson has little background in accounting, but is a very astute businessperson. He calls you in and says, "This year we spent $50,000 to count our inventory. This seems like a waste of money if the accountants are doing their job properly. Why do we need a count when your records should have this information?"

Prepare a memorandum that clearly answers Mr. Wilson's question.[10]

Exercise 9-6
(Intermediate)

As a member of the technical staff of your CPA firm, you receive a request from a member of the audit staff for assistance in determining how to account for a large inventory of one of your clients. The company involved is a manufacturing firm that makes custom-designed machine parts. There are only two other companies in the country with the technology to produce these parts. Your client's firm is the largest of the three. Management has built a reputation not only in the quality of its products but also in customer service. One of the most successful policies it follows is always to manufacture a larger quantity of a part than a customer orders. The extra parts are kept in inventory so that if the customer later has an emergency need for the part, several may be shipped in a matter of two or three hours. The customers don't know that extra parts are being inventoried and therefore think that your client stops all other production to respond to the emergency. This greatly impresses customers and because of this, the customer service business has grown tremendously.

The problem is that any given customer will rarely, if ever, use this service. As a consequence, your client has built a huge inventory of production overruns, and only a small indeterminable amount of it is likely to be used. Your client does not show the inventory on the balance sheet because of its practice to expense the extra cost of production overruns as part of the cost of the production sold. A very large warehouse devoted entirely to this inventory is shown on the balance sheet, however, and is depreciated assuming a twenty-year life.

Write a memo to Mr. Y. Doit of the audit staff stating your position as to how to account for this inventory; deal with any other ramifications you may perceive. Your position should be formed after a *thorough* research of GAAP.[11]

Exercise 9-7
(Intermediate)

The following three independent sets of facts relate to (1) the possible accrual or (2) the possible disclosure by other means of a loss contingency.

Situation I

A company offers a one-year warranty for the product that it manufactures. A history of warranty claims has been compiled and the probable amount of claims related to sales for a given period can be determined.

Situation II

Subsequent to the date of a set of financial statements, but prior to the issuance of the financial statements, a company enters into a contract that will probably result in a significant loss to the company. The amount of the loss can be reasonably estimated.

Situation III

A company has adopted a policy of recording self-insurance for any possible losses resulting from injury to others by the company's vehicles. The premium for an insurance policy for the same risk from an independent insurance company would have an annual cost of $2,000. During the period covered by the financial statements, no accidents involving the company's vehicles resulted in injury to others.

Required:

Discuss the accrual and/or type of disclosure necessary (if any) and the reason(s) why such disclosure is appropriate for one of the three independent sets of facts above.*

Choose Situation I, II, or III. Prepare your answer in the form of a memorandum to the controller of the company for which you work.

Exercise 9-8
(Intermediate)

Cranium Products Company manufactures a variety of sports headgear, which it sells to hundreds of distributors and retailers.

A company "cash clerk" processes all cash received in the mail (mostly checks from customers on account). He opens the mail, sending to the accounting department all accompanying letters and remittance advices that show the amounts received from each customer or other source. The letters and remittance advices are used by the accounting department for appropriate entries in the accounts. The clerk sends the currency and checks to another employee, who makes daily bank deposits but has no access to the accounting records. The monthly bank statements are reconciled by the accounting department, which has no access to cash or checks.

The sales manager has the authority for granting credits to customers for sales returns and allowances, and the credit manager has the authority for deciding when uncollectible accounts should be written off. However, a recent audit revealed that the cash clerk had forged the signatures of the sales manager and the credit manager to some forms authorizing sales allowances and bad debt write-offs for certain accounts. These forms were then sent to the accounting department, which entered them on the books and routinely posted them to customers' accounts.

How could the cash clerk have used these forgeries to cover an embezzlement by him? Assume there was no collusion with other employees. Be specific.[12]

Write a memo to the president of Cranium in which you discuss this situation.

Exercise 9-9
(Intermediate)

Milton Corporation entered into a lease arrangement with James Leasing Corporation for a certain machine. James's primary business is leasing and it is not a manufacturer or dealer. Milton will lease the machine for a period of three years, which is 50 percent of the machine's economic life. James will take possession of the machine at the end of the initial three-year lease and lease it to another, smaller company that does not need the most current version of the machine. Milton does not guarantee any residual value for the machine and will not purchase the machine at the end of the lease term.

Milton's incremental borrowing rate is 10 percent and the implicit rate in the lease is 8½ percent. Milton has no way of knowing the implicit rate used by James.

---

*Material from Uniform CPA Examination Questions and Unofficial Answers, copyright © 1977 by the American Institute of Certified Public Accountants, Inc., is adapted with permission.

Using either rate, the present value of the minimum lease payments is between 90 percent and 100 percent of the fair value of the machine at the date of the lease agreement.

Milton has agreed to pay all executory costs directly and no allowance for these costs is included in the lease payments.

James is reasonably certain that Milton will pay all lease payments, and, because Milton has agreed to pay all executory costs, there are no important uncertainties regarding costs to be incurred by James.

Required:

With respect to Milton (the lessee) answer the following:

1. What type of lease has been entered into? Explain the reason for your answer.
2. How should Milton compute the appropriate amount to be recorded for the lease or asset acquired?
3. What accounts will be created or affected by this transaction and how will the lease or asset and other costs related to the transaction be matched with earnings?
4. What disclosures must Milton make regarding this lease or asset?*

You are a staff accountant of the Milton Corporation. Write a memo to the controller, Helen Garcia, in which you answer these questions.

Exercise 9-10 (Cost)

A supplier to an automobile manufacturer has the following conversation with the manufacturer's purchasing manager:

SUPPLIER: You did not predict the heavy demands. To keep up with your unforeseen demands over the coming quarter, we will have to work six days per week instead of five. Therefore, I want a price increase in the amount of the overtime premium that I must pay.

MANUFACTURER: You have already recouped your fixed costs, so you are enjoying a hefty contribution margin on the sixth day. So quit complaining!

Should the supplier get an increase in price?[13] Write your answer in the form of a memo to the president of the automobile manufacturing firm.

Exercise 9-11 (Cost)

The Thomas Company is in the process of developing a revolutionary new product. A new division of the company was formed to develop, manufacture, and market this new product. As of year end (December 31, 19XX) the new product has not been manufactured for resale; however, a prototype unit was built and is in operation.

*Material from Uniform CPA Examination Questions and Unofficial Answers, Copyright © 1978 by the American Institute of Certified Public Accountants, Inc., is adapted with permission.

Throughout 19XX the new division incurred certain costs. These costs include design and engineering studies, prototype manufacturing costs, administrative expenses (including salaries of administrative personnel), and market research costs. In addition, approximately $500,000 in equipment (estimated useful life—10 years) was purchased for use in developing and manufacturing the new product. Approximately $200,000 of this equipment was built specifically for the design development of the new product; the remaining $300,000 of equipment was used to manufacture the preproduction prototype and will be used to manufacture the new product once it is in commercial production.

Required:

In accordance with Statement of Financial Accounting Standards No. 2, how should the various costs of Thomas described above be recorded on the financial statements for the year ended December 31, 19XX?*

You are the controller of the Thomas Company. Write a memo to the president, Ruth Richards, in which you answer this question. Explain your answer in terms of SFAS No. 2.

Exercise 9-12 (Auditing)

A competent auditor has done a conscientious job of conducting an audit, but because of a clever fraud by management, a material fraud is included in the financial statements. The fraud, which is an overstatement of inventory, took place over several years, and it covered up the fact that the company's financial position was rapidly declining. The fraud was accidentally discovered in the latest audit by an unusually capable audit senior, and the SEC was immediately informed. Subsequent investigation indicated the company was actually near bankruptcy, and the value of the stock dropped from $26 per share to $1 in less than one month. Among the losing stockholders were pension funds, university endowment funds, retired couples, and widows. The individuals responsible for perpetrating the fraud were also bankrupt.

After making an extensive investigation of the audit performance in previous years, the SEC was satisfied that the auditor had done a high-quality audit and had followed generally accepted auditing standards in every respect. The commission concluded that it would be unreasonable to expect auditors to uncover this type of fraud.

Required:

State your opinion as to who should bear the loss of the management fraud. Include in your discussion a list of potential bearers of the loss, and state why you believe they should or should not bear the loss.[14]

Write your discussion in the form of a memorandum to a partner in your firm.

*Material from Uniform CPA Examination Questions and Unofficial Answers, Copyright © 1978 by the American Institute of Certified Public Accountants, Inc., is adapted with permission.

Exercise 9-13 (Auditing)

As part of the analytical review of Mahogany Products, Inc., you perform calculations of the following ratios:

Ratio	Industry 19X6	Averages 19X5	Mahogany 19X6	Products 19X5
1. Current ratio	3.3	3.8	2.2	2.6
2. Days to collect receivables	87	93	67	60
3. Days to sell inventory	126	121	93	89
4. Purchases—accounts payable	11.7	11.6	8.5	8.6
5. Inventory—current assets	.56	.51	.49	.48
6. Operating earnings—tangible assets	.08	.06	.14	.12
7. Operating earnings—net sales	.06	.06	.04	.04
8. Gross margin percent	.21	.27	.21	.19
9. Earnings per share	$14.27	$13.91	$2.09	$1.93

For each of the ratios above:

a. State whether there is a need to investigate the results further and, if so, the reason for further investigation.

b. State the approach you would use in the investigation.

c. Explain how the operations of Mahogany Products appear to differ from those of the industry.[15]

Write your answers in the form of a memo to the auditor in charge of this review.

Chapter 10

REPORTS

One form of writing that accountants often prepare is the written report. A report usually involves analysis of an accounting problem and application of accounting principles to a particular situation. It may also require some research of the professional literature, so the research techniques discussed in Chapter 11 are often part of a report's preparation.

Reports will vary in length, but all reports should meet certain basic criteria. The accounting content should be accurate, the format and organization should be correct, the report should be presented attractively, and the writing style should be effective.

FORMAT

Reports differ from other writing in that they are organized into a set format or structure. Actually, there are a variety of report formats, but they are all designed to make the report easy to read. The format presented in this handbook is typical of the ways in which reports are structured.

A report will likely include the following parts:

letter of transmittal
title page

table of contents
list of illustrations (optional)
introduction
initial summary and/or recommendations
body of the report
conclusion
appendices (optional)
notes
bibliography

Letter of Transmittal.[1]*   The letter of transmittal may actually accompany the report, or it may be mailed separately. This letter is a cover letter; it presents the report to the person for whom it was written and makes whatever comments are necessary to explain its purpose and contents.

The first paragraph of the letter refers to the occasion of the report or explains why you wrote it. Mention the title somewhere in the first paragraph.

The second paragraph includes any other comments about the report that you wish to make. For example, the second paragraph may mention the report's scope, purpose, or limitations, and you may wish to give credit for any special assistance you received in its preparation.

The final paragraph is conventional; it expresses your hope that the report is satisfactory.

Before you write the letter of transmittal, review the discussion of business letters in Chapter 8.

Title Page.   In a report prepared in a professional situation, the title page may look something like this:

Title of Report
Prepared by . . .
Prepared for . . .
Date

In a student report, more information is helpful.

Title of Report
Student's Name
Course and Period
Instructor
Date

---

*Adapted from *Technical Writing,* 4th Edition, by Gordon H. Mills and John A. Walter. Copyright © 1970, 1962 by Holt, Rinehart and Winston. Copyright © 1954 by Gordon H. Mills and John A. Walter. Reprinted by permission of Holt, Rinehart and Winston, CBS College Publishing.

Table of Contents.   The table of contents should be on a separate page and should have a heading. The contents listed will be the major parts of the report, excluding the letter of transmittal, with the appropriate page numbers.

List of Illustrations.   The list of illustrations, if applicable, will include titles and page numbers of graphs, charts, and other illustrations.

Introduction.[2]*   The introduction should be no more than one or two paragraphs. It should contain the following information:

1. Identify the subject of the report. You may also want to give some background information about your topic, such as the definition, theory, or history of the subject, but only if these topics contribute to the purpose of the report or help the reader to understand it. The background of the subject can also be the first division of the report's body.
2. Identify the purpose of the report. The purpose may be combined with the subject identification in one sentence.
3. If necessary, define the scope, or limits, of the report so that the reader will know how much to expect. For example, is the report a general survey or a detailed study? Is it written from a particular point of view?
4. Outline the plan of development near the end of the introduction. You may use a sentence such as this one:
    This report will be divided into five major parts: (1) _____, (2) _____, ...
5. You may want to include in your introduction a statement of the report's importance or value. Consider here the readers' interests, needs, and attitudes.

Initial Summary and/or Recommendation.   This section summarizes the report's main ideas and any recommendations that you wish to make. Note that the summary gives the report's main *ideas,* not the plan of development or major divisions of the body. Write summaries simply; save complex and technical aspects of the report for the body or appendices.

Body of the Report.   Divide the body of the report into appropriate sections and give each section a heading. Transitions in addition to headings are frequently necessary to show the relationships of the various sections.

Conclusion.   In addition to the initial summary, the report should have a final conclusion, with a heading. The conclusion may be quite brief, particularly in a short report. Its purpose is to bring the paper to a close.

Appendices (optional).   Depending on the report's audience and purpose, you may want to place highly technical information, statistics, etc., in appendices at the end of the report. If you use an appendix, give it a title and refer to it in the body of the report.

NOTES AND BIBLIOGRAPHY FOR REPORTS WITH DOCUMENTED RESEARCH

These sections of the report should appear on separate pages, each with a heading. Follow the sample entries given in Chapter 11 for proper form, including correct spacing and margins. Remember that the bibliographical entries should be in alphabetical order.

GRAPHIC ILLUSTRATIONS

Graphic illustrations such as tables, charts, or graphs can sometimes make a report more interesting and informative. If you include such illustrations, give them a descriptive title and briefly summarize their significance within the text. They may be included in the body of the report or in an appendix.

HEADINGS[3]

Frequent headings can make a report easier to read and more attractive to look at. Headings can have a variety of styles, but they must be used in a certain order when there are different levels of division. In other words, some headings indicate major sections of a paper, while other headings indicate minor divisions. Here are four heading styles and the levels of division.

First Level: Centered, Underlined
Second Level: Centered, Not Underlined

Third Level: Left Margin, Underlined
Fourth Level: Left Margin, Not Underlined

If you use fewer than four levels, your headings may be in any style, as long as they are in descending order. For example, you might use second-level headings for main topics and fourth-level headings for subtopics.

APPEARANCE

It is important that you present your report as attractively as possible. Use good quality paper and be sure that the report is neatly typed. Corrections should be few and unobtrusive.

Reports should be double-spaced, with the exception of the letter of transmittal and any set-off material. Pages should be numbered, beginning with the table of contents.

The student report included at the end of this chapter illustrates the techniques of effective report writing.[4]

125 Easy Street
Athens, Georgia
August 8, 19XX

Mr. John Ehrlich
Zealous Corporation
1890 Monroe Drive
Atlanta, Georgia   30306

Dear Mr. Ehrlich:

In response to your request, dated July 21, 19XX, I have
assembled information about convertible debt to assist you in
your financing decision. The accompanying report, entitled
Financial and Accounting Considerations in Issuing Convertible
Debt, examines the nature of convertible debt, the pros and cons
of such an issue, and the accounting treatment of the securities.

As you proposed, I have given some discussion to the
accounting standards (GAAP) affecting convertible debt. Two
Opinions of the Accounting Principles Board, Nos. 14 and 15, have
particular bearing on convertible debt; each is logical, but the
logic of one is quite inconsistent with the logic of the other.

I believe that you will find the standards interesting, and
I hope that my report will meet your needs.

Sincerely yours,

Jean Bryan

jhw

FINANCIAL AND ACCOUNTING CONSIDERATIONS
IN ISSUING CONVERTIBLE DEBT

BY

JEAN BRYAN

ACCOUNTING 501
PERIOD 3-4, M-W

DR. ENGSTROM

AUGUST 8, 19XX

CONTENTS

INTRODUCTION

The purpose of this report is to provide information about an increasingly popular form of financing: convertible debt. Convertible debt is an issue of debt securities (bonds) that carry the option of exchange for equity securities (usually common stock).

While it is hoped that any potential issuer of convertible debt will benefit from this discussion, the report intends primarily to present the accounting requirements in the area of convertible debt, and to promote an understanding of the reasons for those requirements.

Four major topics make up the report: (1) Nature of Convertible Bonds, (2) Financial Advantages and Disadvantages, (3) Accounting Treatment, and (4) Logic of the Accounting Requirements.

INITIAL SUMMARY

Many corporations can benefit from convertible debt, especially corporations which want to obtain low-cost funds now, and desire also to increase their equity in the future. However, firms considering convertible debt financing should be aware of the hardships that may arise from conversion or from non-conversion; they should also be aware that accounting requirements impose a potentially unfavorable presentation of such debt in the financial statements.

NATURE OF CONVERTIBLE BONDS

When convertible bonds are issued, the bond indenture specifies a period of time after issuance during which the bonds may be converted. The indenture also specifies a conversion price, "the amount of par value of principal amount of the bonds exchangeable for one share of stock."[1] If a conversion ratio, rather than a conversion price, is specified, the effective price of stock to the bondholder may be determined by dividing the par value of the bond by the number of shares exchangeable for one bond.

The conversion price, which is determined when the bonds are sold, is usually from 10 to 20 percent above the prevailing market price of the common stock at the time of issue. Both the issuing firm and the investor expect that the market price of the stock will rise above the conversion price, and that the conversion privilege will then be exercised by most or all bondholders.

The indenture typically includes a call provision so that the issuing firm can force bondholders to convert. Therefore, it is evident that firms issuing convertible debt often truly want to raise equity capital. The reasons that they choose convertible debt are discussed below.

FINANCIAL ADVANTAGES AND DISADVANTAGES
Advantages

The use of convertible debt has advantages over straight debt or stock issues. I will discuss the advantages over straight debt first.

Bonds that are convertible into stock, even if the quality of the bond is not very high, are in demand. Therefore, bond buyers are willing to accept a low stated interest rate on such bonds, be willing to pay a premium and accept a lower yield, or accept less restrictive covenants. The issuing firm thus obtains funds at a lower cost than would be possible if the firm issued bonds without the conversion privilege.

The advantages of a convertible bond issue over a common stock issue relate to timing. The firm is willing to take on more equity in the future, but is reluctant to sell stock under present conditions. For example, if the price of the firm's stock is temporarily depressed,

> to sell stock now would require giving up more shares to raise a given amount of money than management thinks is necessary. However, setting the conversion price 10 to 20 percent above the present market price of the stock will require giving up 10 to 20 percent fewer shares when the bonds are converted than would be required if stock were sold directly.[2]

If fewer shares are given up in the long run, then earnings per share will be higher in the long run. In the short run, convertibles do not dilute earnings per share; nor do they lower the market price of new stock issues of similar size.

Another possible advantage of convertibles, related to the number of shares given up, is the retention of certain ownership interests. For example, one stockholder may own most of the stock and want to maintain control. He may be able to do so by voting against a large issue of stock, advocating instead the issue of bonds which are convertible into a number of shares small enough not to injure the stockholder's majority.

Disadvantages

Most of the disadvantages of convertibles are related to the uncertainty of the conversion and its timing. If the stock price does not rise, conversion will not occur, and the issuing firm will not obtain the equity financing it desired. The firm might then have difficulty meeting the unplanned-for obligations of debt. On the other hand, if the price of the common stock increases, the issuing firm might have been better off to wait and sell the common stock.

Other disadvantages arise when the conversion occurs. When the debt becomes equity, earnings per share is reduced, operating leverage is reduced, and income taxes rise because interest expense is reduced.

ACCOUNTING TREATMENT

The Accounting Principles Board, in its Opinion No. 14, ruled that convertible bonds "which are sold at a price or have a value at issuance not significantly in excess of the face amount"[3] must be treated in the same manner as other bonds. That is, "no portion of the proceeds from the issuance . . . should be accounted for as attributable to the conversion feature."[4] The expectation that some or all of the bonds will be converted into stock is given no recognition in the accounts.

Since convertibles are normally sold at a premium, the amount of the cash proceeds from the issue is greater than the face value of the bonds. The difference between the debit to Cash and the credit to Bonds Payable is credited to a Premium on

Bonds account. The premium is amortized, using the effective interest method, over the life of the bonds. The effect of the amortization is that the interest expense recorded by the firm each period does not equal the amount of the interest payment, but reflects the effective yield to the bondholders.

When bonds are converted, the firm removes from the accounts the balances associated with those bonds: Bonds Payable is debited for the par value of the bonds converted, and the Premium account is debited for the portion of the unamortized premium which is attributable to the bonds converted. Two methods exist for recording the common stock issued in exchange for the bonds. Under one method, the stock is assigned a value equal to the market value of the stock or the bonds. If this value differs from the book value of the bonds (the balances associated with the bonds, mentioned above), then a gain or a loss is recorded. Under the other method, which is more widely used, the value assigned to the stock equals the book value of the bonds, and no gain or loss is recognized or recorded.[5]

If the issuing firm retires its convertible bonds for cash before their maturity date, the transaction is recorded in the same way as the early retirement of any other debt. The difference between the book value of the bonds and the cash paid to retire them is a gain or a loss. If the gain or loss is material, it is shown as an extraordinary item on the income statement.

While convertibles are accounted for solely as debt, accountants must consider the equity characteristics of such issues in computing earnings per share (EPS). APB Opinion No. 15

requires that corporations which have issued securities that are potentially dilutive of EPS must present, in their financial statements, two EPS figures. If a convertible security meets the requirements of certain tests, it is considered a common stock equivalent and enters the calculation of primary EPS; otherwise, it enters only the calculation of fully diluted EPS.[6]

Both EPS figures represent EPS <u>as if</u> the bonds had been converted into stock. If they had been converted, the removal of the bonds would have caused a reduction of interest expense, which would have increased earnings; therefore, the accountant revises the earnings, as well as the number of shares, upward.[7] However, the positive effect of the earnings adjustment may not offset the negative effect of the shares adjustment. The result is that convertibles reduce reported EPS.

LOGIC OF THE ACCOUNTING REQUIREMENTS

In requiring that convertible debt be accounted for solely as debt, the APB reasoned that the debt and the conversion feature are inseparable.[8] That is, at any given time, a security is either all debt or all equity. Therefore, since at the time of issuance the security is all debt, its issuance should be recorded as debt.

The Board argued further that practical problems exist in the attempt to value the debt and conversion features separately. The conversion feature is difficult to value because of the uncertainty of the timing of conversion, and because of the uncertain future market value of the stock. The debt part of the security is difficult to value independently of the conversion option, because the conversion option affects the terms of the bond. An attempt to value the bonds as if they were not convertible would require the assumption of higher terms--an unrealistic assumption, because the issuing firm would not have wanted to issue bonds with those terms.[9]

The accounting requirements concerning presentation of EPS are intended to meet investors' reporting needs. In its Opinion No. 15, the APB explains that the value of a convertible security "is derived in large part from the value of the common stock to which it is related," and that the holder of such a security is essentially a participator in "the earnings and earnings potential of the issuing corporation."[10] Therefore, the determination of EPS based only on outstanding shares of common stock "would place form over substance,"[11] and would mislead the investors.

CONCLUSION

In the decision whether to finance with convertible debt, a firm must consider whether its situation would benefit from using convertibles rather than straight debt or stock issues, and whether it can meet the debt requirements, should conversion not occur as expected. In addition, management should analyze carefully the effect of the issue on readers of the financial statements, because until the bonds are converted, a possibly high level of debt will exist alongside a lowered presentation of earnings per share.

Notes

[1]Jules I. Bogen, ed., Financial Handbook, 4th ed. (New York: Ronald Press, 1968), p. 31.

[2]Eugene F. Brigham, Fundamentals of Financial Management (Hinsdale, Ill.: Dryden Press, 1978), p. 532.

[3]Accounting Principles Board, Accounting for Convertible Debt Issued with Stock Purchase Warrants, Opinions of the Accounting Principles Board No. 14 (New York: American Institute of Certified Public Accountants, 1969), para. 1.

[4]Ibid., para. 10.

[5]Donald E. Kieso and Jerry J. Weygandt, Intermediate Accounting, 3rd ed. (New York: John Wiley & Sons, 1980), p. 715-16.

[6]Ibid., p. 736-37.

[7]Ibid., p. 737-38.

[8]Accounting Principles Board, Opinion No. 14, para. 10.

[9]Ibid., para. 6.

[10]Accounting Principles Board, Earnings Per Share, Opinions of the Accounting Principles Board no. 15 (New York: American Institute of Certified Public Accountants, 1969), para. 25.

[11]Ibid., para. 26.

WORKS CITED

Accounting Principles Board. Accounting for Convertible Debt and
    Debt Issued with Stock Purchase Warrants. Opinions of the
    Accounting Principles Board No. 14. New York: American
    Institute of Certified Public Accountants, 1969.

Accounting Principles Board. Earnings per Share. Opinions of the
    Accounting Principles Board No. 15. New York: American
    Institute of Certified Public Accountants, 1969.

Bogen, Jules I., ed. Financial Handbook. 4th ed. New York:
    Ronald Press, 1968.

Booker, Jon A., and Jarnagin, Bill D. Financial Accounting
    Standards: Explanation and Analysis. Chicago: Commerce
    Clearing House, 1979.

Brigham, Eugene F. Fundamentals of Financial Management.
    Hinsdale, Ill.: Dryden Press, 1978.

Kieso, Donald E., and Weygandt, Jerry J. Intermediate Accounting.
    3d. ed. New York: John Wiley & Sons, 1980.

NOTES

1. The information in this section is based on Gordon H. Mills and John A. Walter, *Technical Writing*, 3rd ed. (New York: Holt, Rinehart and Winston, Inc., 1970), p. 359.

2. The information in this section is based on Mills and Walter, *Technical Writing*, pp. 254–57.

3. The information in this section is based on Kate L. Turabian, *A Manual for Writers of Term Papers, Theses,* and *Dissertations*, 4th ed. (Chicago: The University of Chicago Press, 1973), pp. 7–8. Adapted from *A Manual for Writers of Term Papers, Theses and Dissertations*, pp. 7–8, by Kate L. Turabian, by permission of the University of Chicago Press. © 1937, 1955, 1967, 1973 by the University of Chicago.

4. Jean Bryan, "Financial and Accounting Considerations in Issuing Convertible Debt" (unpublished student paper, University of Georgia, 1980).

5. Malcolm H. Lathan, "Writing Assignment for Intermediate Accounting" (unpublished class assignment, University of Georgia, 1982).

6. Gordon S. May, "Writing Assignment for Intermediate Accounting" (unpublished class assignment, University of Georgia, 1982).

7. Randolph A. Shockley, "Writing Assignment for Intermediate Accounting" (unpublished class assignment, University of Georgia, 1982).

8. James Don Edwards, Johnny R. Johnson, and Roger A. Roemmich, *Intermediate Accounting* (Plano, Texas: Business Publications, Inc., 1981), p. 26.

9. Roger A. Roemmich, "Writing Assignment for Intermediate Accounting" (unpublished class assignment, University of Georgia, 1982).

10. Adapted from Charles T. Horngren, *Introduction to Financial Accounting* (Englewood Cliffs, N.J.: Prentice-Hall, Inc., © 1981), p. 112. Reprinted by permission.

11. Alvin A. Arens and James K. Loebbecke, *Auditing: An Integrated Approach*, 2nd ed. (Englewood Cliffs, N.J.: Prentice-Hall, Inc., © 1980), p. 73. Reprinted by permission.

EXERCISES

Write reports for the following situations. Invent any details you need to make the reports complete.

Exercise 10-1
(Intermediate)

You are employed as a special assistant to Mr. Joseph Uga, president of Bulldog Sales Company. Mr. Uga's twenty-five-year-old son, Bubba, a recent graduate of Preppy Community College, has just been hired as vice-president of sales. Bubba's major career objective is early retirement. He recently called you in for a chat. "You know," he said, "a friend of Dad's at the Second National Bank of Vidalia told me last week that if I deposit $2,000 per year in one of their individual retirement accounts (IRA), I'll be able to retire as a millionaire in thirty years. I don't understand how he can make an offer like that. Can you tell me if he's on the level?"

Prepare a report for Bubba that clearly explains how the banker can make this claim.[5]

Exercise 10-2
(Intermediate)

You have received an inquiry from a prospective client, Johnson Marketing, Inc., concerning the accounting for inventories. Johnson is in the process of establishing a very large mail order business that will require a large inventory of miscellaneous items to be sold at different markups. Write a report for this client explaining briefly the various options of accounting for inventories and their effects. Remember that your client is *not* an accountant and knows very little about accounting.[6]

Exercise 10-3
(Intermediate)

Smith and Jones are planning to open a new downtown shoe store. Smith has heard of the FIFO, LIFO, specific identification, and lower-of-cost-or-market methods of valuing inventory, but does not understand them. Since you will be the accountant for the partnership, Smith has asked you to prepare a report recommending an appropriate method for valuing the inventory. Jones has asked that the report describe the advantages and disadvantages of each method, from both practical and theoretical perspectives.[7]

Exercise 10-4
(Intermediate)

Reedy Enterprises has recently engaged you to help prepare the accounting records necessary prior to making a public offering of stock. Reedy has not previously prepared accounting records in accordance with GAAP.

a. How will you determine what GAAP is appropriate for the industry in which Reedy operates?
b. Differentiate between primary and secondary sources for establishing GAAP.
c. Reedy will be selling securities in several states. What impact might this fact have upon the presentation of its financial statements?[8]

Write a report for Reedy in which you answer these questions.

Exercise 10-5
(Intermediate)

Southeastern Enterprises, an association of real estate developers, has contacted your firm. The association is interested in your position on the recognition of income from the sale of development properties. While there is considerable variation within the association, a typical contract has a down payment of 5 to 15 percent. Remaining payments may be spread over many years.

The managing partner of your firm has asked you to write a report on recognition of income from land development sales. This report will be distributed to the real estate developers who make up Southeastern Enterprises.[9]

Exercise 10-6
(Intermediate)

Valuation of assets is an important topic in accounting theory. Suggested valuation methods include the following:

- historical cost (past purchase prices)
- historical cost adjusted to reflect general price-level changes
- discounted cash flow (future exchange prices)
- market price (current selling prices)
- replacement cost (current purchase prices)

Required:

a. Why is the valuation of assets a significant issue?
b. Explain the basic theory underlying each of the valuation methods cited above. Do not discuss advantages and disadvantages of each method.*

Prepare your answers in the form of a report to the Board of Directors of Elwood Manufacturing Co.

Exercise 10-7
(Intermediate)

Hanover Company and Case Company, both of which have only voting common stock, are considering a merger whereby Hanover would be the surviving company. The terms of the combination provide that the transaction would be carried out by Hanover's exchanging one share of its stock for two shares of Case's stock. Prior to the date of the contemplated exchange, Hanover had purchased five percent of Case's stock, which it holds as an investment. Case, at the same date, owns two percent of Hanover's stock. All of the remaining outstanding stock of Case will be acquired by Hanover in this contemplated exchange. Neither of the two companies has ever had any affiliation as a subsidiary or division of any other company.

Required:

Based only on the facts above, discuss the specific criteria that would qualify or disqualify this business combination to be accounted for as a pooling of interests.

*Material from Uniform CPA Examination Questions and Unofficial Answers, copyright © 1979 by the American Institute of Certified Public Accountants, Inc., is adapted with permission.

What additional requirements (other than those discussed above) must be met in order to account for this business combination as a pooling of interests?*

Prepare your answer in the form of a report to Sandra Stephens, president of Hanover.

Exercise 10-8
(Intermediate)

The following are the summarized transactions of Dr. Cristina Faragher, a dentist, for 19X7, her first year in practice:

1. Acquired equipment and furniture for $50,000. Its expected useful life is five years. Straight-line depreciation will be used. Assume no salvage value.
2. Fees collected, $80,000. These fees included $2,000 paid in advance by some patients on December 31, 19X7.
3. Rent is paid at the rate of $500 monthly, payable on the twenty-fifth of each month for the following month. Total disbursements during 19X7 for rent were $6,500.
4. Fees billed but uncollected, December 31, 19X7, $15,000.
5. Utilities expense paid in cash, $600. Additional utility bills unpaid at December 31, 19X7, $100.
6. Salaries expense of dental assistant and secretary, $16,000 paid in cash. In addition, $1,000 was earned but unpaid on December 31, 19X7.

Dr. Faragher may elect either the cash basis or accrual basis of measuring income for income tax purposes, provided that she uses it consistently in subsequent years. Under either alternative, the original cost of the equipment and furniture must be written off over its five-year useful life rather than being regarded as a lump-sum expense in the first year.

1. Prepare a comparative income statement on both the cash and accrual bases, using one column for each basis.
2. Which basis do you prefer as a measure of Dr. Faragher's performance? Why? What is the justification for the government's allowing the use of the cash basis for income tax purposes?[10]

You are on the staff of the CPA firm that is preparing Dr. Faragher's income statement. Write a report for Dr. Faragher that includes items 1 and 2.

Exercise 10-9 (Auditing)

The Lakeland Milk Products Company is a medium-sized company engaged in purchasing unpasteurized milk and processing it into different dairy products. For the past six years Lakeland has had services performed by a CPA firm, which includes audit services, tax services, and management consulting services. Since Lakeland lacks a competent controller, a major part of the fee has consisted of

*Material from Uniform CPA Examination Questions and Unofficial Answers, copyright © 1977 by the American Institute of Certified Public Accountants, Inc., is adapted with permission.

correcting the accounting records, making adjusting entries, and preparing the annual financial statements. Recently, the president of Lakeland asked the CPA in charge of the Lakeland audit for the past three years if he would be interested in becoming the full-time combination controller and internal auditor for the company.

Required:

    a.   Which services currently being provided by the CPA firm could be done by the CPA acting in his new capacity, assuming he is qualified to perform them?

    b.   Which services must the CPA firm continue to perform, even if the new controller is qualified? Why must they be done by the CPA firm?

    c.   Explain specific ways the controller can help reduce the CPA's audit fee if he is knowledgeable about the way the audit is conducted.[11]

Prepare your answer in the form of a report to the president of Lakeland.

Chapter 11

RESEARCH PAPERS

Sometimes accountants need to research the professional accounting literature as one step in the preparation of a report or memo. This research may involve an in-depth look at official pronouncements, such as the Opinions of the Accounting Principles Board (APB) or Statements of the Financial Accounting Standards Board (FASB). Sometimes, too, accountants must research the details of government regulations, such as provisions of the Internal Revenue Code. And occasionally accountants need to read other kinds of professional literature, such as journal articles or monographs on topics of current interest.

This chapter discusses, in an elementary, step-by-step approach, how to write a research paper. Much of the material will be review for students or professionals who have written term papers or documented reports. However, the suggestions should be helpful to anyone who must research the professional literature and then summarize the results of that research in a written form.

HOW TO START

If you are writing a paper that requires research of the literature, chances are you already know something about the topic. If you don't, or if your memory is only vague, do some initial reading so that you have a basic familiarity with your subject. An accounting textbook may be a good place to start.

Once you have a general idea of what your topic involves, you will need to look for additional information. Many times the next step will be to look at official accounting pronouncements, such as those found in *Accounting Standards: Current Text.*[1] Or you may need to study government regulations or laws to find out how to handle a client's technical problem. For either case, read the material carefully and take accurate notes of your findings, including references to the sources you are using. A later section of this chapter discusses note taking in more detail.

Some research papers will require a search for additional source materials in the library. The subject files of the card catalog can direct you to books written on your topic. Remember, too, that books on a broader subject than you are researching may have chapters or sections on your topic. For example, if your topic is transfer pricing, you might find some information in a book on cost accounting.

Much of the information you find in the library will probably come from periodicals, rather than books. The *Accountants' Index*[2] lists articles published in accounting periodicals. The index is arranged chronologically in volumes covering perhaps half a year. Within each volume, the articles are grouped according to topic and author. Be imaginative in looking for articles on your topic; consider the different headings it could be listed under. For example, "Stock rights" might be listed as "Fractional share rights," "Share rights," or "Stock warrants."

After you have noted any books or articles that may be useful in your research, ask the librarian to help you find what you need. He or she may direct you to the stacks for books and bound volumes of periodicals, or you may need to use the library's microfilm files.

NOTE TAKING

Once you have located a useful source, take notes on what you read. For this step in your research you will need two sets of cards—3 × 5″ cards for the bibliography and 4 × 6″ (or 5 × 8″) cards for the notes. Using these cards will save time and trouble in the long run, even though they may seem like a bother at the time you are reading. They will help you keep track of your sources and notes, and they will be easy to use when you write your rough draft.

Let's look first at a bibliography card.

Horngren, Charles T. Introduction to Financial Accounting. Englewood Cliffs, N.J.: Prentice-Hall, Inc., 1981.

BIBLIOGRAPHY CARD

Be sure that you include on the card all the information you will need for your bibliography (see "Documentation," pages 151–152). It's frustrating to make an extra trip to the library just to check on a date or volume number.

Note cards contain the information you will actually use in your paper.[3]

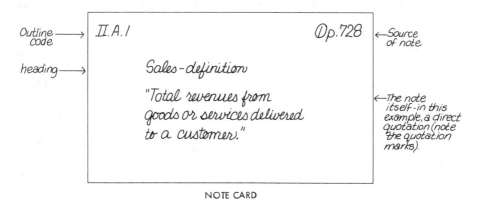

NOTE CARD

Notice the parts of the note card. The numbers in the upper right-hand corner give the source (from the bibliography card) and the page(s) where this information was found. The heading gives you an idea of what this note card is about. The note itself is taken from the source. It is the material you will use in your paper.

DIRECT QUOTATION AND PARAPHRASE

You can take notes in two ways, as direct quotation (the exact words from the source) or as paraphrase (your words and sentence structures). It is usually much better to take the notes in your own words. If you take the time to paraphrase as you research, you'll save time when you write your rough draft.

Here's a good way to paraphrase. Read a section from your source—perhaps several short paragraphs. Then look away from the page and try to remember the important ideas. Write them down. Then look back at your source to check your note for accuracy.

Occasionally you may want to use a direct quotation. When you copy a quotation on a note card, use quotation marks so you'll know later that these are someone else's words. Copy the quotation *exactly,* including capitalization and punctuation.

It is important that direct quotations be accurate and that paraphrases be your own words and sentence structures, not just a slight variation of your source.

THE OUTLINE

As you are taking notes, you will probably form some idea of the major divisions of the paper. That is, you should be getting a rough idea of its outline.

Go ahead and write down your ideas for an outline. The more reading you do, the more complete the outline will become. Stop and evaluate the outline from time to time. Are you covering all the important areas of your topic? Is the outline getting too long? Should you narrow the topic? Are some sections of the outline irrelevant to the topic? Answering these questions will guide you as you continue your research.

Once your research is complete, or nearly so, you should refine your outline. Be sure that your topic is covered completely and that the ideas are arranged in the most effective order. Think about the introduction and conclusion to your paper, and any other relevant parts. For example, do you want to include charts, tables, or graphs?

Next, arrange the note cards in the order of the outline. It is a good idea to write the outline code in the upper left-hand corner of the card.

With a completed outline and an orderly stack of note cards, you are ready to write the rough draft.

THE ROUGH DRAFT

The rough draft of a research paper is written just like that of any other kind of writing (see Chapter 2), with the exception that you are incorporating note cards into your own ideas. If you've already paraphrased the notes, your task is much easier.

You do need to include in your rough draft an indication of where your notes came from. In other words, you want to give credit for words or ideas that are not your own. In the final version of your paper, these references will be the footnotes or endnotes. In the rough draft, you can indicate your sources with a parenthetical notation like this: (① p. 728). The numbers come from the note card and refer to the source and page number of the note.

It is important that you give credit for every idea not your own. If you don't, you will be guilty of plagiarism. *The Harbrace College Handbook* contains the following discussion of plagiarism:

> If you fail to acknowledge borrowed material, then you are plagiarizing. Plagiarism is literary theft. When you copy the words of another, be sure to put those words inside quotation marks and to acknowledge the source with a footnote. When you paraphrase the words of another, use your own words and your own sentence structure, and be sure to give a footnote citing the source of the idea. A plagiarist often merely changes a few words or rearranges the words of the source. As you take notes and as you write your paper, be especially careful to avoid plagiarism.[4]

Writers sometimes plagiarize without intending to, because they don't understand how to paraphrase. The following sentence comes from an accounting text:

> Financial reporting should also provide information about changes in financial resources which result from financing and investing activities.[5]

The next sentence illustrates how a writer might plagiarize; this sentence is too close to the source:

> Another objective of financial accounting is to provide reliable information about changes in net financial resources which result from the financing and investing activities of an enterprise.

REVISING

After you have completed the rough draft of your research paper, you will need to revise it to perfect the organization, development, style, grammar, and spelling. Review Chapter 2 for a discussion of revision.

DOCUMENTATION

Any information you get from another source must be documented. Footnotes or endnotes are usually used for student papers; parenthetical notes within the text itself are usually used for scholarly publications. Most authorities consider endnotes, which are easiest to write and type, quite acceptable. When you use documentation of any kind, you will usually need a bibliography.

One widely accepted authority for note and bibliography style is Kate L. Turabian's *A Manual for Writers*.[6] You may want to buy a copy to use as you write your papers.

Here are some sample entries for typical accounting sources. Make your notes and bibliographies complete and accurate, including punctuation.

BIBLIOGRAPHY AND NOTES

Book
N. [1]DONALD E. KIESO AND JERRY J. WEYGANDT, *Intermediate Accounting* (2nd ed.; Santa Barbara: John Wiley & Sons, 1977), p. 173.
B. KIESO, DONALD E., AND WEYGANDT, JERRY J. *Intermediate Accounting*. Santa Barbara: John Wiley & Sons, 1977.
Article in a Journal
N. [2]ALFRED RAPPAPORT, "The Strategic Audit," *Journal of Accountancy* 149 (June 1980): 72.
B. RAPPAPORT, ALFRED. "The Strategic Audit." *Journal of Accountancy* 149 (June 1980): pp. 71–77.
Article in a Magazine
N. [3]BARBARA SWANSON, "Competition in Accounting," *Atlantic*, September 1973, p. 85.
B. SWANSON, BARBARA. "Competition in Accounting." *Atlantic*, September 1973, pp. 83–87.

APB Opinion
N.   [4]Accounting Principles Board, *Disclosure of Lease Commitments by Lessees,* Opinions
      of the Accounting Principles Board No. 31 (New York: American Institute of Certified
      Public Accountants, 1973), para. 8.
B.   Accounting Principles Board. *Disclosure of Lease Commitments by Lessees.* Opinions
      of the Accounting Principles Board No. 31. New York: American Institute of Certified
      Public Accountants, 1979.
FASB—Financial Accounting Standard
N.   [5]Financial Accounting Standards Board, *Disclosure of Information About Major Cus-
      tomers: An Amendment of FASB Statement No. 14,* Statement of Financial Accounting
      Standards No. 30 (Stamford, Connecticut: Financial Accounting Standards Board,
      1979), para. 7.
B.   Financial Accounting Standards Board. *Disclosure of Information About Major Custom-
      ers: An Amendment of FASB No. 14.* Statement of Financial Accounting Standards
      No. 30. Stamford, Connecticut: Financial Accounting Standards Board, 1979.
FASB—Financial Accounting Concept
N.   [6]Financial Accounting Standards Board, *Objectives of Financial Reporting by Business
      Enterprises,* Statement of Financial Accounting Concepts No. 1 (Stamford, Connecti-
      cut: Financial Accounting Standards Board, 1978), para. 33.
B.   Financial Accounting Standards Board. *Objectives of Financial Reporting by Business
      Enterprises.* Statement of Financial Accounting Concepts No. 1. Stamford, Connecti-
      cut: Financial Accounting Standards Board, 1978.
FASB—Discussion Memorandum
N.   [7]Financial Accounting Standards Board, *Conceptual Framework for Financial Account-
      ing and Reporting: Objectives of Financial Reporting by Nonbusiness Organizations,*
      FASB Discussion Memorandum (Stamford, Connecticut: Financial Accounting Stan-
      dards Board, 1978), p. 3.
B.   Financial Accounting Standards Board. *Conceptual Framework for Financial Account-
      ing and Reporting: Objectives of Financial Reporting by Nonbusiness Organizations.*
      FASB Discussion Memorandum. Stamford, Connecticut: Financial Accounting Stan-
      dards Board, 1978.
AICPA—Statement of Position
N.   [8]American Institute of Certified Public Accountants, *Recognition of Profit on Sales of
      Receivables with Recourse,* Statement of Position 74-6, rpt. in *Statements of Position
      of the Accounting Standards Division as of January 1, 1978* (Chicago: Commerce
      Clearing House, Inc., for the American Institute of Certified Public Accountants,
      1978), para. 10,010.02.
B.   American Institute of Certified Public Accountants. *Recognition of Profit on Sales of
      Receivables with Recourse.* Statement of Position 74-6. Rpt. in *Statements of Position
      of the Accounting Standards Division as of January 1, 1978.* Chicago: Commerce
      Clearing House, Inc. for the American Institute of Certified Public Accountants, 1978.
Accounting Research Study
N.   [9]Oscar S. Gellein and Maurice S. Newman, *Accounting for Research and Development
      Expenditures,* Accounting Research Study No. 14 (New York: American Institute of
      Certified Public Accountants, Inc., 1973), p. 14.
B.   Gellein, Oscar S., and Newman, Maurice S. *Accounting for Research and Development
      Expenditures.* Accounting Research Study No. 14. New York: American Institute of
      Certified Public Accountants, Inc., 1973.
Primary Source Quoted in *Accounting Standards*
N.   [10]Financial Accounting Standards Board, *Objectives of Financial Reporting by Business
      Enterprises,* Statement of Financial Accounting Concepts No. 1, rpt. in *Accounting
      Standards: Current Text* (Stamford, Connecticut: FASB, 1982), Sec. 1210.

B.   Financial Accounting Standards Board. *Objectives of Financial Reporting by Business Enterprises*. Statement of Financial Accounting Concepts No. 1. Rpt. in *Accounting Standards: Current Text*. Stamford, Connecticut: FASB, 1982.

NOTES

1.   Financial Accounting Standards Board, *Accounting Standards: Current Text* (Stamford, Connecticut: FASB, 1982).
2.   Jane Kubat, ed., *Accountants' Index* (New York: American Institute of Certified Public Accountants).
3.   Information on note card quoted from Charles T. Horngren, *Introduction to Financial Accounting* (Englewood Cliffs, N.J.: Prentice-Hall, Inc., © 1981), p. 728. Reprinted by permission.
4.   John C. Hodges and Mary E. Whitten, *Harbrace College Handbook*, 8th ed. (New York: Harcourt Brace Jovanovich, Inc., 1977), p. 372.
5.   James Don Edwards, Johnny R. Johnson, and Roger A. Roemmich, *Intermediate Accounting* (Plano, Texas: Business Publications, Inc., 1981), p. 9.
6.   Kate L. Turabian, *A Manual for Writers of Term Papers, Theses, and Dissertations*, 4th ed. (Chicago: The University of Chicago Press, 1973).

EXERCISE

Choose one of the following topics, and narrow it if necessary. (For example, you might select "Careers in Government Accounting" rather than "Careers in Accounting.") Write a documented research paper on your topic, using the steps discussed in this chapter.

1.   History of the Accounting Profession
2.   Public- *vs*. Private-Sector Regulation of Accounting
3.   Accounting for the Effects of Inflation
4.   Careers in Accounting
5.   Accounting for Leases
6.   Accounting for Oil and Gas Exploration
7.   Computers and Accounting
8.   Accountants in the F.B.I.

INDEX